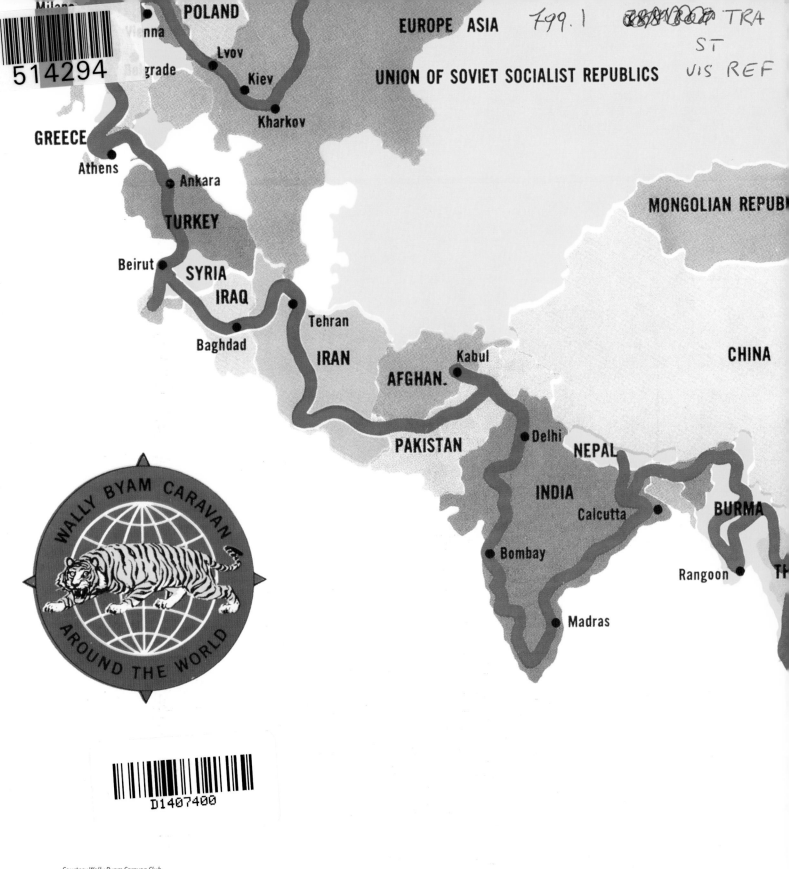

Milano

POLAND

Vienna

EUROPE ASIA 799.1 TRA
ST
VIS REF

Lvov

Belgrade

Kiev

UNION OF SOVIET SOCIALIST REPUBLICS

Kharkov

GREECE

Athens

Ankara

MONGOLIAN REPUB

TURKEY

Beirut

SYRIA

IRAQ

Tehran

Baghdad

CHINA

IRAN

Kabul

AFGHAN.

PAKISTAN

Delhi

NEPAL

WALLY BYAM CARAVAN

INDIA

BURMA

Calcutta

AROUND THE WORLD

Bombay

Rangoon

TH

Madras

*Courtesy Wally Byam Caravan Club
International (the Airstream RV Association).*

Home away from Home

The World of Camper Vans and Motorhomes

Edited by Kate Trant

Black Dog Publishing

Contents

Introduction *Pioneering Spirits*　7

Kate Trant

Terms of reference	8
The authors	8
Motorised RVs	9
Towable RVs	9

Chapter One *Of Comfortable Gypsies and Grey-haired Rebels*　11

Lars Eriksen

How the motor became a home	12
On the road	15
Home is where the car is	17
The boom years	19
Vagabond diaries	22
High life	24
Hip to be on board	32
The modern way	36
Tin can trash	42
Road dreams	43
Endnotes	44

Chapter Two *No Place Like Home*　45

Kate Trant

Home comforts	47
Uncharted territory: freedom and independence	48
Contemporary tin can tourists	55
For one night only	57
Free to go	64
Flying south for the winter	71
Excess baggage	72
American dreams	74
Euro visions	76
Roll your own	82
Worlds collide or worlds apart?	101
Strange bedfellows	107
Home cooking	108
Endnotes	110

Chapter Three All Mod Cons 111

Malcolm Bobbitt

Mobile developments	112
Airstream Classic	118
Auto-Sleepers Clubman	120
Bedford Dormobile	122
Bessacarr E700 Range	125
Bluebird Highwayman	127
Calthorpe Home Cruiser	128
Caraversions HiTop	130
Ci Autohomes Highwayman	131
Citroën H Type	132
Coachmen Leprechaun	134
Country Coach Inspire 360	135
Danbury	136
Fiat Amigo	138
Fiat 600D	140
Ford Transit	142
Holiday Rambler Vacationer	144
Hymer	146
Knaus Traveller	149
Moto-Caravan	150
National RV Tropi-cal	152
Niesmann+Bischoff ClouLINER	154
Rapido	156
Romahome	157
Sportmobile	158
Suntrekker	160
Toyota Hi-Ace	162
Volkswagen Transporter	166
Winnebago	170

Chapter Four Compact Living 175

Kate Trant

Design and mobility	176
A place for everything and everything in its place	178
Getting away from it all	186
Of no fixed abode?: perceptions and reality	188
Carrying the world on your back	190
Minimal living	192
Design, motorhomes and campervans now	198
Endnotes	202

References	203
Clubs	205
Acknowledgements	207

Introduction

Pioneering Spirits

Kate Trant

The spirit of independent automotive travel over the last 100 years or so has often been captured by the VW Bus. But from the Dormobile, Devon and Danbury, through Fleetwood and Holiday Rambler, to Westfalia and Winnebago, the range of camper vans and motorhomes across the USA, UK and beyond is vast. In some, we find travel at a basic, sparsely equipped level while, at the other end of the spectrum, contemporary motorhomes are spectacularly well fitted, with more technology and equipment than many homes, and prices to match.

This book outlines the cultural and social history of the camper van and motorhome in the USA, UK, Europe and further afield, looking at a range of phenomena from surf and hippy culture, to family holidays and travel in retirement years. In Chapter One, Lars Eriksen offers a historical context that will look at the desire for mobility as part of a pioneering spirit, including journeys by covered wagon in the mid-Western USA in the mid nineteenth century. The role of the motorhome as the vehicle for an 'alternative' lifestyle will be looked at; this will include the phenomenon of bus conversions—Ken Kesey and his Merry Pranksters, and surf culture through one of its most lasting icons—the VW Bus.

Whether about a pioneering spirit, large horizons and wide, open spaces, economic travel or a comfortable change of scenery, what is common to camper or motorhome owner is the need to create a "home away from home". Camper van and motorhome owners are sometimes seen as inhabiting very different worlds rather than two ends of the same spectrum. But is there not just a little bit of wanderlust in every motorhome or camper driver? Chapter Two looks at the contemporary culture of camper van and motorhome to see if there is any common ground between them and illustrates the culture, style and philosophy of camper van and motorhome travel with stories of road trips, adventures and journeys from across the USA, UK and Europe.

In Chapter Three, Malcolm Bobbitt looks at a range of camper vans and motorhomes through the twentieth century to the present day, within the context of the technical developments and design approaches that dictate their appearance, as well as some of the ways in which they were marketed to the buying public.

Chapter Four explores future possibilities for independent camper van and motorhome travel, alongside contemporary approaches to 'compact living', drawing parallels between motorhome culture and the many non-automotive trappings of a modern urban lifestyle, from Walkmans and ipods to Wi-Fi and rucksacks.

Terms of Reference

Definitions of motorhome and camper vary from country to country, at times related to legislative differences, at others to a general and more intangible cultural understanding. This book will be using the terms 'camper van' and 'motorhome', occasionally referring to 'RV' in the US. The term 'camper van' will be used to describe vehicles such as the VW bus and others that fit broadly into the same category. While the book will refer to caravan design and culture, in the main the vehicles examined in detail will be motorised rather than towable.

The vehicles presented in Chapter Three represent a small sample of the vast range of motorhomes and camper vans available now and in the past worldwide. We are aware that each individual reader will readily make their own personal selection and there will probably be as many different selections as there are readers of this book. However, deciding the criteria for selection, we took the decision to present only vehicles that could be illustrated which, occasionally, meant ruling out a small selection of desirable vehicles for whom illustrations proved too elusive.

The Authors

Lars Eriksen is a journalist and freelance writer.

Malcolm Bobbitt is the author of *VW Bus Type 2: Camper, Van, Pickup, Wagon,* 2001, *Bubble Cars and Microcars,* 2003, *Taxi! The Story of the 'London' Taxicab,* 1998, and *Three Wheelers: Those Were the Days,* 2003.

Kate Trant is co-author of *The Macro World of Microcars,* 2004 and curator of *Moving Objects: Thirty Years of Vehicle Design at the Royal College of Art,* 1999.

The book uses the definition of RV as defined by the RVIA. There are two major categories of RV: "Motorised RVs' and 'Towable RVs'.

Motorised RVs ▶

Type A Motorhome

Generally roomiest of all RVs, sleeping up to six, and with luxury amenities.

Type B Motorhome

Commonly called 'van campers' in the US, they sleep up to four and drive like a family van.

Type C Motorhome

With optional sleeping space over the cab, Type Cs sleep up to eight and have similar amenities to Type As.

Towable RVs ▶

Folding Camping Trailer

Sleeping up to eight, these fold for lightweight towing.

Truck Camper

Mount on a pickup bed or chassis and sleep up to six.

Conventional Travel Trailer

With a wide range of floor plans and sizes available, trailers can sleep up to ten.

Fifth-wheel Travel Trailer

Towed with a pickup truck and sleep up to six.

Travel Trailer with Expandable Ends

Lightweight towing with ends that pull out for roomy sleeping.

Sport Utility RV

Motorised or towable (as travel trailers or fifth-wheels), with a built in 'garage' for sports equipment.

Chapter One

Of Comfortable Gypsies and Grey-haired Rebels

Lars Eriksen

How the motor became a home

From retired millionaires to hippies who had never given up on the nomad dream, they all shared a passion for the mobile lifestyle...

I lost my camping virginity in the shadows of South Dakota's Black Hills with the dead presidents on Mount Rushmore watching over me. I couldn't have asked for a more romantic setting. The campground reached as far as your eyes could glimpse through the hazy blur of the sun clashing with aluminium shells. VW bus conversions slotted into overhangs in the hilly sections while monstrous Airstream motorhomes ruled the ground. The plan was to use this north-eastern portal to explore the Wild West, but I quickly realised that the world outside the campground had to take a backseat to the new community of campers and RV enthusiasts that we had joined. Mornings were spent in communion at the pancake buffet and in the afternoons my Canadian neighbours would keep me entertained with stories from a lifetime aboard a campervan. At the same time the Stetson-clad full-timers across the gravel path would light up their Texan barbecue. It was a diverse crowd. From retired millionaires to hippies who had never given up on the nomad dream, they all shared a passion for the mobile lifestyle and in the morning they all dumped their black toilet water in the same tank. Aside from the unforgettable experience of sipping cocktails in a million-dollar motorhome (in the company of Mr and Mrs Johnson from San Fernando Valley rather than Mötley Crüe) the feeling of being part of a mobile community was truly exceptional. It left me with an impression of a society free of geographical or political barriers but bound by the realisation of a mobile existence. It is a notion recognised by the author Warren James Belasco who, in his studies of how America fell in love with life on the road in the early part of the twentieth century, has summed up the remarkable synergy between tent plugs and egalitarianism that arose in the early twentieth century and transcended socio-economic divides: "Here was a true melting pot, a regenerative social harmony of which every host town could be proud."[1]

*George E McFadden from Mesa, Arizona,
flips pancakes at the WBCCI Hobo Rally in
Blythe, CA, in February 2001.
Photograph by Jenny Nordquist.*

On the road

The ambition of a home on the road is inextricably linked to the exploration of America's vast landscape and the pioneering spirit, which has been a consistent trait of the American condition. Since Lewis and Clark's first expeditions in the early 1800s to map out the western terrain there has been an urge for people to uproot and explore a nation polarised by geographical barriers. The aspiration of a better life has fed a lust for travel and Americans have carried their homes on their backs since the pioneers trekked to the bright wide fields of the Pacific coast. To these pioneers who travelled the dusty and muddy tracks across the continent, the physical challenges of the nation were not facts but questions to which they set out to find the answers. Because of the great distances and the arduous and primitive conditions of the roads, the western third of the United States at the time "might just as well have been located on a separate continent".[2] Between 1841 and 1857 more than 165,000 people migrated to California by land and thousands more headed north-west to Oregon.[3] In a move to counter the British domination of the Oregon country in the early nineteenth century, expansionists had been highlighting the desirability of the region to the public. In 1822 the Virginia Congress representative John Floyd hailed the region as a treasure trove of furs and fuelled the notion of Oregon as an attractive destination prompting ambitious fur traders and explorers to follow the congressman's prophecies. The surge that this generated drew up the path for the Oregon Trail, the 2,000-mile long pioneer pipeline which became one of the central migration routes. Thousands of people travelled along the trail from Missouri to Oregon with their packed wagons

and prairie schooners, helping America to realise its goal of 'manifest destiny'—the belief that the nation had a divine mission to expand across the north American frontier. The historical importance of the pioneers' legacy was not lost on the modern traveller as a caravan enthusiast noted in 1969:

> As a hangover from the old days [when the old pioneers discovered that wagon drivers who banded together stood the best chance of crossing the prairies with their scalps intact], the nomadic wanderer of today hauling his aluminium wagon still shares a rapport for his fellows which transcends all levels and knows no class distinction.[4]

Scotts Bluff, NE, Oregon National Trail.
Courtesy of the National Park Service.

Ford Model T.
© Ford Motor Company and
Wieck Media Services, Inc.

The California gold rush in the middle of the nineteenth century further catalysed improvements in the infrastructure and transport facilities of the West. On 10 May 1869 the Central and the Union Pacific Railroads finally completed the nation's first transcontinental rail connection, marking a drastic and fundamental change to the way Americans could travel. For the pioneers that had travelled with their wagons along the Oregon Trail, the transcontinental journey could take up to half a year, whereas the railroad could expedite people across the country in a matter of days. The railroad would remain the most common means of transportation up until the early part of the twentieth century but the invention of the automobile at the turn of the century was the pivotal catalyst for the aspiring vagabond. A new breed of affluent individualists saw in the car the possibility to escape from the constraints of the industrialised metropolis. It was an attractive alternative offering a new sense of freedom from the physical limitations of the railcar and the peculiarities of fellow passengers. Echoing Rousseau's rejection of the restrictions of time (a gesture later echoed by Dennis Hopper

and Peter Fonda in their iconic counterculture adventure *Easy Rider*) the car provided independence most directly from the constraints of timetables and cramped railroad cars. But more importantly, it hailed a new approach to travel that truly cultivated the innate pioneering spirit. The car travelled off the beaten track, opened up new roads, relationships and knowledge. It nurtured human relations across social and cultural divides and broke the railroad's "monopolistic hold over American geographical consciousness".[5] But adventure came at a price. The first cars were expensive and the road surface was still crude and often unegotiable for the humble machines. All that changed in 1908 when Henry Ford introduced the world to his Model T, which not only revolutionised car travel and made it affordable to the masses but also initiated a manufacturing and cultural revolution that would change the fabric of American society.

Home is where the car is

Despite the grass and dirt-covered tracks—in 1900 only about 150,000 miles of public roads in America were 'paved' with crude materials like stone and gravel—people took to the roads with unbridled passion. The Lincoln Highway would not connect the nation from coast to coast until the 1930s but even when the first muddy trails were laid out in 1913 it greatly stimulated public interest in the possibilities of transcontinental car travel. Industrialisation took its toll on the urban inhabitant and prompted a desire for a return to nature inspired by the gypsies that toured Britain in horse-drawn wagons around the turn of the century. These imaginative 'auto-gypsies' were dictated by a primitive 'call of the wild' and helped domesticate the roads along with hobos, traders and outdoor enthusiasts who attached tents to their cars during extended fishing and hunting trips. The gypsy aspiration was an important factor in the car's transition from a means of transport to shelter. Moreover, their international associations and family-orientated lifestyle would also find their way into the new 'domestic' car culture.

Despite the early aspirations, factory-produced cars had little power and resilience and were therefore useless for roadside shelter. Up until the late 1920s most just had folding tops and translucent, snap-on side curtains that offered limited protection from the harsh weather conditions. The seats did not move or fold and were not even wide enough to use as a sleeping quarter. But on both sides of the Atlantic innovative and ambitious travellers attempted the marriage between the car and domestic space while manufacturers began to produce cars that were specifically made for sleeping and dining. In 1910 Pierce-Arrow Motor Car Company's 6 cylinder touring landau went on show in New York. Furnished with camping appointments, tooled leather upholstery and equipped with a folding washbasin, toilet and a water tank, it was a prestigious and luxurious acquisition at $8,250 (by that time a Ford Model T cost $950). Not surprisingly, the affluent owners

Arthur Rothstein, Lincoln Highway, Pennsylvania, 1941. Library of Congress, Prints and Photographs Division, FSA-OWI Collection, reproduction number, LC-USF34-024502-D.

were enjoying the touring experience from the backseat while communicating with their private chauffeurs via a telephone link. The Pierce-Arrow generated an appreciative community of owners who experimented in making modifications to the functionality of their vehicles, fitting iceboxes instead of the washbasin and compartments for cutlery and crockery.

Notwithstanding the primitive condition of the road network, British automobile and camping enthusiasts were keeping up with American ingenuity and the appetite for a home on the road. The British railway exercised a similar monopoly on holiday travel up until the combustion engine started its reign. Although by 1904 there were only 8,465 private cars in the UK, there was already a keen interest in camping and motor caravan travel which was reflected in the formation of the Caravan Club in 1907.[6] Early motorhome manufacturers such as Belsize Motor Company and Eccles Motor Transport Company understood the need to address motorhome space. From the earliest experimentation of sleeping in cars to the modern day RV parks—where people decorate their motorhome and campsite territory with all the panache and attentiveness of any suburban neighbourhood—there has always been a desire to transpose the environments of home onto the mobile platform. This was exemplified by the popularity of the lavish 'house cars' that first hit the roads at the start of the century. They were custom built bodies out of wood, fibre board, metal and canvas placed on a car chassis, often audacious and extravagant but, at times, almost comical in their desire to fit out what looked like normal houses with four wheels. The house car was significant in the evolution towards fulfilling the dream of a comfortable home on the road—a mobile extension of everyday life with the accessories necessary for the family to feel at ease and at home while still benefiting from a proximity to nature and gypsy romanticism.

This desire was never more obvious than with Roland R Conklin's Gypsy Van in 1915. Conklin was a bus executive whose career had been boosted by the progress of the automobile, and his 25 foot, eight-ton vessel was an exercise in elegance and efficiency at the time. The two-story vehicle had 44 windows and an upper deck fitted with a folding top, side curtains and a motorcycle. The interior was in the style of an English country mansion with large furniture and paintings recreating a familiar home décor that was almost camp in its excess.[7]

The Gypsy Van influenced the design of camping vehicles for years to follow. But because of the costs involved in building these elaborate machines they were mostly the toys of the privileged few—most of whom had affiliations with the automobile industry. Their size and lavishness was similar to the railroad cars but they were longer, more powerful and better fitted. Their owners were oil barons and truck executives who experimented with large bus chassis fitting them out with gadgets like radios and electric fans. One of the most famous owners was Will Keith Kellogg—the man behind Cornflakes—who toured America offering cereal samples in his dark-blue Ark made out of aluminium and based on a White Model 50 chassis. It was fitted out with swivel chairs in taupe mohair, mahogany panels and Spanish leather upholstery and carried a 16 foot folding boat behind it.

The boom years

The roadside changed its face to the beat of the Jazz Age when living in vehicles became a trend and campgrounds, restaurants and billboards began to crop up in the landscape. In 1925 the US government realised their ambitions for a public highway system and the route that ran from Chicago to Los Angeles, and which would become part of American cultural folklore, was christened Route 66. The flat trail ran through the big southern states and linked together small towns from the Midwest to the Pacific coast. The improvements to the road network boosted the interest in auto-camping. In a country separated by natural boundaries, camping life became a common socio-cultural denominator whereby travellers united in explorations beyond that which was familiar to them. In 1919 a group of autocampers met at Desota Park in Tampa, Florida and formed the Tin Can Tourists. They organised rallies and conventions across the country and were always recognisable by the tin can that was soldered on the radiator of the members' cars. In the early 1920s there were between 3,000 and 6,000 campgrounds across America and in the 1930s, the Tin Can Tourist membership soared to over 100,000. The rise in facilities was not simply for the benefit of the camper or the product of an altruistic consideration for conservation. Auto-camping had become a commercial potential and campgrounds lured people with amenities such as water wells, communal lounges and bathrooms. These new 'luxuries' signalled a move away from the original Gypsy dream to a consumerist desire for the comforts of modern living attached to the nomadic lifestyle. Primitivism for the traveller, as Belasco notes, is a split between the more ascetic notion of endurance associated with the pioneers' hardship and suffering and a more hedonistic 'Garden of Eden'.[8]

The democratic mantra of the campground was tainted by a wish to get rid of the 'undesirable' elements in municipal parks, causing towns to impose fees, time limits and police supervision in order to attract only the more affluent and 'better class' tourists. People had started using the

Dorothea Lange, *Billboard on US Highway 99 in California*, 1937. Library of Congress, Prints and Photographs Division, FSA-OWI Collection, reproduction number LC-USF34-016211-C.

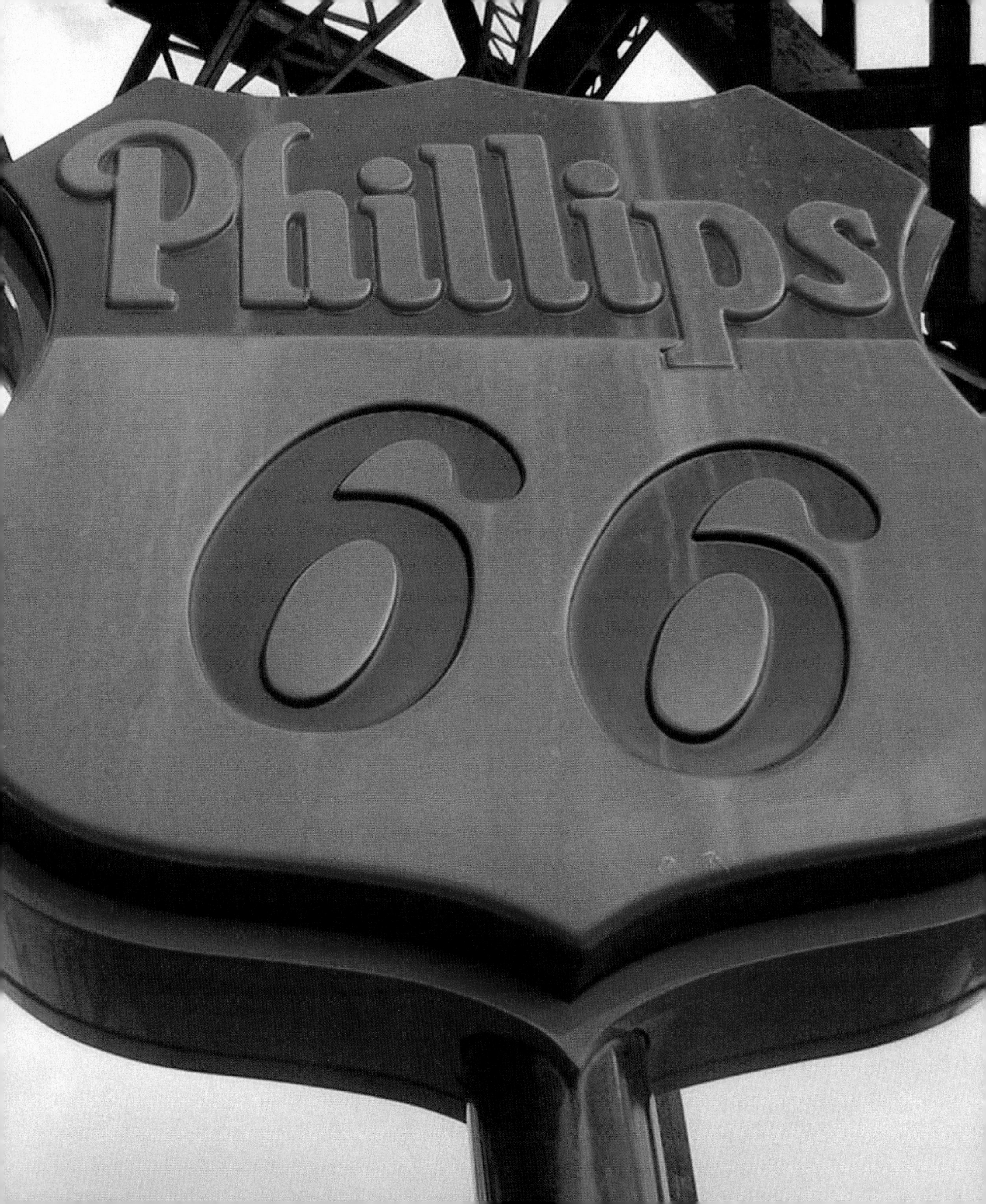
Phillips
66

campground and the highway as their permanent and free residence, which caused apprehension towards the vagabond lifestyle. Writers, poets and entertainers made the roadside their home and their stage. Continuing the age-old tradition of the strolling minstrels and travelling companies, shows took to the road, including the Ringling Brothers who toured the country with 107 20 yard carriages and freight wagons transported on four trains while Charles G Phillips' production of *Uncle Tom's Cabin* rolled along in an ornate house car decorated with stained glass and silk drapes. Such extraordinary grandeur was rarely found in the surroundings of the everyday car traveler. Nevertheless, customisation and modification became a popular activity.

In Britain people started experimenting beyond the standard Ford chassis, which had enjoyed a small monopoly because of the accessibility to spare parts and servicing. An article in *The Austin Magazine* introduced the idea of a micro motorhome by converting an Austin Seven into a comfortable sleeping quarter while the Cara-Bed by Weathershields Ltd in Birmingham had a fold-out unit attached to the rear of the car that could sleep two. Around 1928 Land Yachts Ltd in Middlesex conceived of the Light Cruiser—a luxurious motorhome that stood out from its contemporaries with its streamlined design. The interior included a cooker, shower, full-sized toilet, gramophone and a cigar lighter and it could be fitted onto any chassis with an engine over 20 hp. The Light Cruiser never made it into production but its strangely seductive shape marked a striking departure from the bulky motorhomes of the early twentieth century. Of this more spectacular and voluptuous breed, the vision of grandeur of the mobile hunting lodge that Harrington Ltd of Hove in the UK produced for Captain JF Macmullen almost matched Conklin's Gypsy Van in decadence and style. This two-storey motorhome built on an AEC Regal bus chassis not only had a full-sized cooker and fridge but also a sundeck. Like many other heavy duty motorhomes of its time, the Hunting Lodge had to avoid soft ground because of its weight. Nevertheless it often covered up to 150 miles a day when the Captain took it on tours around Scotland.[9]

In 1927 the Phillips Petroleum Company of Battlesville named its gasoline Phillips 66, a reflection of public excitement about the building of Route 66, and developed a logo to match.

This two-storey motorhome built on an AEC Regal bus chassis not only had a full-sized cooker and fridge but also a sundeck. As many other heavy duty motorhome of its time the Hunting Lodge had to avoid soft ground because of its weight. Nevertheless it often covered up to 150 miles a day when the Captain took it on tours around Scotland.

Vagabond diaries

The lust for life on the road generated a culture of writing in the shape of diaries, literature and articles by travelling journalists who combined their journeys with reporting. The language reflected the spirit of autonomy and the wanderlust that was symptomatic of the time and expressed a romantic and almost transcendental aspect of motoring. One magazine dubbed the home on the road "Thoreau at 29 cents per gallon" pitching the vagabond lifestyle as exemplifying the key to a truer understanding of life through its marriage between gasoline, nature and the human soul.[10] Life on the road and the return to nature was seen as a liberation of the imagination and greater appreciation of culture. Walt Whitman became an inspirational poet for the auto-gypsies. In *Leaves of Grass*, 1855, he connected the exploration of America with a personal discovery. Motor travel writers found this insight hidden in the lyrical clash between the pulsating motor and romantic experience of the open landscape. As Kris Lackey explains in his analysis of travel literature:

> ... the rhetoric of motor travel transforms the machine at its centre into a prosthesis of consciousness—artificial but so well fitted to the human mind and body that it all but disappears.[11]

This notion can also be discerned in Lewis Sinclair's 1919 novel *Free Air* which follows New York socialite Claire driving her ailing father across the country to Seattle. Sinclair pays tribute to the road adventure as his protagonists navigate mud, dust and gravel while coming to terms with the more fundamental trappings of life. By contrast, in Mary Bedell's record of her and her husband's 12,000 mile clockwise camping journey around the United States, the romantic element is subdued by a more pragmatic approach to her travels yet her description paints a striking picture of the ambitions and realities of auto-camping at the time. While lamenting the conditions of the road system she concludes that the attractions around her trip are not enough to outweigh the advantages of small-town life she nonetheless shares the same optimistic vision of life on the road as Lewis's Claire:

The lure of this unconventional mode of life gets into the blood and one is ready to suffer much discomfort for the opportunity of getting into close touch with the people of this great democracy. There is no better way of discovering the fine traits of our fellow countrymen than by packing up a kit and going a-gypsying.[12]

Magazines also offered the travelling community a forum in which to share hints and tips. In 1924 *Motor Camper and Tourist* began in New York and in 1930 the Motor Camping Club of Britain launched its magazine, the *Motor Camper,* declaring in their mission statement that "the motorcamper is never too selfish to teach and never too clever to learn; the printed word will assist him (and all the 'hims' include 'hers') to do both".[13] The magazine advertised upcoming rallies and meetings, and included a gallery of illustrations of tents dating back to 174AD to show today's camper that he owed "something to the ingenuity of his forebears".

In 1929 the economic bubble burst on Wall Street and the aftershock was visible on the road, which changed from a setting of adventure to an unforgiving trail for the poor and desolated in search of jobs, shelter and a new future. The burgeoning auto-camping scene also suffered a set-back because of the changing social and cultural infrastructure of the roadside environment. The backdrop on the highway was no longer the romantic nomadic ideal of a home on wheels but rather the social realism of the Depression era.

Top: Dorothea Lange, Squatter camp on the outskirts of Bakersfield, California, November 1936. Library of Congress, Prints and Photographs Division, FSA-OWI Collection, reproduction number LC-USF34-009978-C.

One magazine dubbed the home on the road "Thoreau at 29 cents per gallon" pitching the vagabond lifestyle as exemplifying the key to a truer understanding of life through its marriage between gasoline, nature and the human soul.

Middle: Dorothea Lange, Home of a dust bowl refugee in California, Imperial County, March 1937. Library of Congress, Prints and Photographs Division, FSA-OWI Collection, reproduction number, LC-USF34-016263-C.

Bottom: Dorothea Lange, Migratory family in autocamp, California, November 1939. Library of Congress, Prints and Photographs Division, FSA-OWI Collection, reproduction number, LC-USF34-009991-C.

Farmers kept working on the sterile soil when the droughts of the early 1930s worsened, and the Plains winds swept across the fields in the giant Dust Bowl which left thousands of families with ruined crops and huge debts. They took to Route 66 in their beaten-up cars in search of salvation. In John Steinbeck's *The Grapes of Wrath*, 1939, the Joad family heads across the fabled route in pursuit of opportunity on the West Coast. Like many of the real life stories of the time, their journey was a test of survival that highlighted the transport revolution which had transformed during the previous decade. Steinbeck's protagonists were refugees as opposed to the adventurous pioneers that Whitman's nomadic muse had inspired. The characters were not literate idealists and the novel shows a less romantic view of technological progress as the family finds themselves slaves of the machine chronicled in the detailed description of the car and its breakdowns. It was only when the United States entered the Second World War that Roosevelt's New Deal policies started to make a real difference.

High life

The end of the Second World War was anticipated with palpable excitement among the British motor camping community. In June 1945 *Motor Trailer* magazine wrote:

> Soon we shall once more be free to search for wild and lonely spots on the coast; far from boarding houses and hotels. (…) And when that wanderlust for the sea comes upon us there will be no need to worry about restrictions, barbed wire, black-out or petrol coupons for we shall travel by caravan and stop where we will and at our time.[14]

The shortage of materials after the war momentarily stalled production but it would only delay the inevitable boom in the autocamping industry that took place on both sides of the Atlantic. Between the wars, car holidays were reserved for only the most adventurous drivers. In 1939 there were over two million private cars in the UK but only an estimated 17,000 were taken to the continent. However, improvements in the road system helped promote domestic automotive travel and soon the speed limit was increased from 20 mph to 30 mph while motorhomes were reclassified as private vehicle. This development further boosted sales, especially of delivery vans which were now being used as bases for motorhomes. However, the road network still didn't stand up to the new challenge. A survey of British roads in *The Manchester Guardian* in January 1954 addressed the urgent problems of the constricted road system and lamented the inadequate budget expenditure on the issue: "This country has not got the good roads it needs, not because the money is not there, but because of an attitude of mind which puts roads at the bottom of the capital investment budget."[15]

The article applauded the government for recognising the necessity of motorways and hailed the success and extensiveness of the American highway—the "creature (and also the twin, to indulge in a biological enormity) of the motor vehicle". In 1958 Britain's first motorway, the Preston Bypass opened and a year later the first inter-urban motorway, a 72 mile stretch of the M1, linked St Albans with the West Midlands.

Another obstacle for the ambitious British traveller had been the slow and expensive procedure of shipping cars over the English Channel, but the introduction of roll-on, roll-off ferries in the 1950s further opened up Europe for travel. This was thanks, in part, to Captain Townsend back in 1928 whose car had been damaged while being loaded onto a ship. Unable to claim compensation, he decided to set up his own ferry service and acquired a minesweeper which was converted to carry 15 cars and 12 passengers from Dover to Calais. The cars still had to be loaded on to the ferry by crane, but unlike the other cross-channel service, the ferry didn't handle other types of freight and thus made the shipping of cars a much quicker and hassle-free operation. As a consequence, cross-channel car traffic experienced a manifold increase.

Left: Dorothea Lange, Oklahoma dust bowl refugee, San Fernando, California, June 1935. Library of Congress, Prints and Photographs Division, FSA-OWI Collection, reproduction number LC-USF34-002613-C.

Bottom: Travellers buying their GB plate before a trip to the continent. Courtesy the Archives of the Royal Automobile Club, Pall Mall.

Home away from Home The World of Camper Vans and Motorhomes

Travel to and from the continent became more popular and more possible for a wide range of people at the end of the 1950s. All images courtesy the Archives of the Royal Automobile Club, Pall Mall.

In the USA the happy days of the 1950s rekindled the nation's love affair with the car as the trials and tribulations of the war years and the great depression were left behind. The automobile reclaimed its central role in the family as people headed back out to discover a roadside which was turning into a consumerist themepark. At the beginning of the decade there were 1,700 drive-in cinemas, McDonalds sold burger number 1,000,000 and the Rev Robert Schuller opened a drive-in church—'a shopping centre for Jesus Christ'—in Garden Grove, California in 1954.[16] It was the birth of the automotive entertainment parlours that lined highway exits and turned the main drag of most cities into a colourful 'strip' bathed in neon and gargantuan billboards.

The Second World War had put highway construction and the automobile culture in America on ice with car sales falling by 3 million in the first year of the war. It took some time for sales to pick up after the war but by the 1950s output soared. This was assisted by a proliferation of ingenious advertisements as well as by advantageous policies such as the housing act of 1949 which kicked off an 'urban renewal'. The subsequent construction of expressways in cities like New York, Detroit and Chicago established the connection between the new suburbs and the city centres. In 1956 Dwight D Eisenhower helped launch the Interstate Highway System which was the largest public works programme in US history paving the way for over 40,000 miles of highways. The system's ambition reflected the low oil prices and the pressure of the automobile industry. To a certain extent it was also the result of a Cold War aspiration that demanded easy escape routes for evacuations in case of 'Communist bombs'.

With the new and improved terrain, trucks, trailers, buses and motorhomes gained new territory, which generated innovations in production methods. The house cars, which up until then had mostly been the privilege of the very affluent, saw a revival burgeoned by the new streamlined trailer design. The motorhome now became an attractive design object, which drew the attention of a new breed of industrial designers who saw it as a canvas on which to project their ideas. Pilots and engineers returning from the war had already introduced aluminium sheeting and tubular steel frames to create more durable and stronger house cars using aircraft technology.

Dodge Motor Home marketing brochure, 1963.
Collection of Kate Trant.

One manufacturer who learned from his wartime experience was Wally Byam whose Airstream trailer has become an American style icon of the road. After the bankruptcy of the Bowlus trailer company in 1936, Byam picked up the leftovers of the company and its innovative design ideas and created the seminal Airstream Clipper with its round silver-clad shape. During the war, the characteristic aluminium alloy that was the Airstream's magic ingredient became an essential component of the war industries and trailers had to give way to bombers and fighters. Byam was forced to temporarily close his company and work for an aircraft manufacturer in Los Angeles. But by the 1950s he had resumed production of the Airstream, which to this day manufactures some of the most sought-after motorhomes. The iconic trailer was not only at the forefront of design excellence but also generated a unique community amongst its owners. The Wally Byam Caravan Club International, formed in 1955, united trailer owners in a dream of diplomacy that rivalled the League of Nations. The Byam ethos truly revived the pioneering spirit and did much to promote the positive perception of the home on wheels. Byam had always been conscious of the media and the public's inclination to categorise trailer owners: "We are determined to improve our 'public image,' as the boys on Madison Avenue say, so that people change their absurd notion that we are homeless gypsies."[17]

The official Wally Byam creed stresses the importance of playing a part in promoting international "goodwill and understanding among the peoples of the world through person-to-person contact". Byam changed the ambitions of the independent traveller and perhaps anticipated and understood globalisation better than any political thinker could have at the time. In 1956 Byam was escorted though the streets of Havana to meet President Batista and three years later he lead a caravan of 41 trailers through Africa to meet with the emperor of Ethiopia Haile Selassie I.[18] These constitute some of the remarkable images that have fuelled the Airstream legend. It managed to encompass a spirit of worldliness and adventure, creating diplomats who travelled the world, met political leaders and parked in front of the Pyramids. If Byam's motive was to challenge our preconceptions about the mobile home he succeeded beyond expectation.

The Wally Byam Caravan Club International, formed in 1955, united trailer owners in a dream of diplomacy that rivalled the League of Nations. The Byam ethos truly revived the pioneering spirit and did much to promote the positive perception of the home on wheels.

Top: Wally Byam Caravan Club International
members in Mexico, 1955.
Courtesy of the Wally Byam Caravan Club
International (the Airstream RV Association).

Left: Rally at Wisconsin Dells, 1959.
Courtesy of the Wally Byam Caravan Club
International (the Airstream RV Association).

Another American icon that was explored by motorhome entrepreneurs was the Greyhound bus. Travellers increasingly turned toward large-scale bus conversions as they realised the advantages of making simple adjustments to pre-fabricated bodies in order to equip them for touring. It also signalled a change in RV culture from the smaller modified station wagons to larger and more convenient sleeping quarters. Greyhound buses with their ample under-body luggage storage attracted the attention of long-time motorhome enthusiasts Anheuser-Busch (the St Louis brewery which produces Budweiser) and even Elvis Presley who equipped his Greyhound Scenicruiser with a 'sky lounge' in red velvet.[19] One of the leading bus manufacturers in the USA was the Flexible Company of Loudonville, Ohio who responded to the demand for conversions by furnishing some of their intercity buses as luxury buses. These were impressive and expensive affairs costing up to $50,000, but vacationers of modest means who also wanted space and comfort on the road found a more affordable option in converting used transit and school buses. These could be purchased for a few hundred dollars and were practical for larger families who regarded them as a cheap alternative to the motel. As with many other groups of niche motorhomes, owners of converted busses gathered in large organisations, such as the Family Motor Coach Association, and exchanged ideas of how to fit out the interior of their buses and debate their self-contained mobile existence.

Travellers increasingly turned toward large-scale bus conversions as they realised the advantages of making simple adjustments to pre-fabricated bodies in order to equip them for touring.

Hip to be on board

"It was like a boy scout's dream", Ken Kesey told a journalist when his bus full of Merry Pranksters arrived in New York in the summer of 1964 after driving across America introducing people along the way to the hippie aesthetics and the psychological and intellectual potential of hallucinogenic drugs.

LSD-25 (Lysergic Acid Diethylamide-25) had been developed by Swiss chemists in 1938 while looking for the potentially therapeutic effects of the fungus ergot. The initial tests carried out on guinea pigs proved rather futile but when Dr Albert Hofmann returned to the work in 1943 he got his fingers tangled up in test tubes. Not only did he inadvertently take the first human acid trip but he opened the minds of an experimenting generation.

While studying at Stanford University in 1959, Kesey was working at a veterans' hospital were he took part in the MK-ULTRA programme—CIA financed research into the effects of LSD. His experiences at the hospital inspired his 1962 seminal bestseller *One Flew Over the Cuckoo's Nest* while laying the chemical foundation for the transcontinental acid trip in 1964. Together with his cohorts of Merry Pranksters, Kesey converted a 1939 International Harvester school bus into a rainbow-coloured counterculture battleship with the mission of visiting the World Fair in New York City. Along the way he was offering people to take part in the Elektrik Kool-Aid Acid Test, enshrined in literary history with Tom Wolfe's book of the same name. The bus, inconsequently and, perhaps, poetically named 'Furthur', was painted in psychedelic swirls of colours ("the kind of shapes and colours you could hear"), fitted out with a complete sound system, a rooftop stage and a refrigerator stashed with LSD.[20] At the helm sat the Beat icon Neal Cassady who, of course, was the inspiration for Jack Kerouac's Dean Moriarty in *On the Road*. Everybody from Alan Ginsberg to Timothy Leary joined in along the way and the Pranksters even managed to strike a peaceful accord with the Hell's Angels after introducing the notorious bikers to the psychoactive realms of LSD (much to the horror of the journalist Hunter S Thompson who was writing his book about the motorcycle club at the

time and thought the cataclysmic mix of oily denim jackets and beatnik philosophy would prove a dangerous cocktail).[21]

Furthur became the iconic metaphor for a generation. The utilitarian bus conversion, with its 'rapping' captain and portable carnival, distilled the essence of a generation into a mobile dream. Like the early experimental motorist writers and artists who took to the road in search of a novel lyricism, the Pranksters, many of whom were rebelling against their own middle class existence, detached themselves from the social and economic constraints of conventional society. But rather than a merely personal liberation, Furthur generated a romantic epiphany for its protagonist. They kept touring until the late 1960s and their rolling tribute to the counterculture movement inspired other adventures such as the Beatles' Magical Mystery Tour. The notion of a spectacle on wheels can be traced right through to the acid house parties of the 1980s or today's freetekno sound systems which travel around as nomadic tribes arranging impromptu techno music festivals.

During the early 1960s when Southern California embraced the fringe fraternities of the counterculture movement it also became the playground of a burgeoning surf scene. The old Hawaiian tradition became a Californian trend styled in flowery shirts and soundtracked by bands like the Surfaris and The Beach Boys with their innocuous pop harmonies. On the big screen seminal surf films such as *The Endless Summer* glorified the cool clean-cut dude in search of the perfect wave. When surfing culture had a more recent resurgence in the 1980s alongside skate- and snowboarding it was fuelled by the same image of a sun-induced Pacific lifestyle. Another thing that the new generation inherited was the surfers' unrelenting love affair with the Volkswagen bus.

Growing up in Denmark, we knew it as the Rye Bread. In Germany it became the Bulli and in America it's simply The Bus. The VW Transporter's name may never have been set in stone, but just like the timeless silver tan of the Airstream, the VW bus's design, with its shiny happy face and its rectangular body-shape, is a visual trademark. Both surfers

and hippies adapted the bus as a symbol of 'utilitarian excellence'. It could carry a number of people plus camping gear and cooking supplies, extra clothing and do-it-yourself tools. Its boxy, functional shape was uncharacteristic of American cars at the time which could have been seen as a statement against the *status quo*. The absence of a drive shaft and the fact that it sat closer to the ground made it more practical both as a cargo and passenger vehicle. It utilised the basic features of the station wagon and delivery truck but combined it with style and functionality. What really made it stand out was the possibility to convert it for both travel and leisure, something that American manufacturers like Ford, Dodge and Chevrolet tried to emulate but never quite matched. The German caravan manufacturer Westfalia introduced the first conversion kit—the Camping-Box—in 1951 and in Britain Danbury and Dormobile were two of the numerous manufacturers who turned the bus into a motorhome. Volkswagen issued strict guidelines for these conversions, though the company itself never produced a camper body for the Transporter.

VW Camper marketing brochure, 1962.
Collection of Everett Barnes.

Home away from Home The World of Camper Vans and Motorhomes

The modern way

In 1973 GMC advertised its new range as "finally a motorhome that doesn't look like a box or ride like a truck" and suggested that the driver of this vehicle should claim the throne as the "King of the Road".

The oil crisis left its mark on the 1970s with gasoline shortages and price increases that slowed the growth of the motorhome industry and put several manufacturers out of business. But if the economic climate shaded the financial possibilities of the industry it only put a brief damper on the ingenuity of designers and consumer demand. Manufacturers had to roll with the punches and mimicked the car industry's move towards smaller and lighter vehicles, bringing about a renewed focus on the streamlined design. In America, the campervan saw a resurgence in the slipstream of the VW bus's success although some makers of bigger and more luxurious motorhomes wanted to disassociate themselves from the VW's more practical look. In 1973 GMC advertised its new range as "finally a motorhome that doesn't look like a box or ride like a truck" and suggested that the driver of this vehicle should claim the throne as the "King of the Road". It echoed the general feeling that the bigger and bulkier motorhome was the preferred option over motels or towable caravans. The success of another US company, Winnebago—the "Miracle on the Prairie", was testament to this shift in demand. In the late 1960s Winnebago became the USA's best selling motorhome with output soaring from 200 to 65,300 motorhomes per year between 1961 and 1973. In 1992 Winnebago produced its motorhome number 250,000 confirming it as being at the forefront of manufacturers but also manifesting the motorhome as an established leisure vehicle almost a century after people had first tried to take their home on the road.

Dodge Motor Home marketing brochure, 1963. Collection of Kate Trant.

Winnebago first showed its face in the UK at the Earl's Court motor show in 1971 at a time when motorhome sales were booming. *Continental Autocamping* lamented the "self converted delivery vans which are piled high with junk and full of long haired youths" but acknowledged the acceptance of the motorhome as not only a viable travel alternative but also a prestigious one: "the modern 'autocamper' should no longer be associated automatically with rugged outdoor individuals or unkempt students bumming their way around Europe in a 1934 Austin-7. Like the damp tent, those days are over."[22]

British motorhome manufacturers turned increasingly toward the coach-build option because it provided more space and better quality. Although today they face stiff competition from other European manufacturers, makers such as Auto-sleepers have insured that the British motorhome industry has managed to keep up with a growing market.

Right: Dodge Motor Home marketing brochure, 1963.
Collection of Kate Trant.

Opposite: Desert Center, California, USA, February 2001.
Photograph by Jenny Nordquist.

Home away from Home The World of Camper Vans and Motorhomes

The senior RVers' life on the road has become interdependent with the community that is cultivated through clubs and rallies, such as the annual gathering in Quartzite, Arizona, where a town the size of about 2,000 people is taken over by more than a million motorhomes and caravans.

While motorhome travel has positioned itself as an accepted and desirable leisure activity, the last 30 years have seen the birth of a new community of motorhome enthusiasts who have committed themselves to living on the road. The phenomenon of 'snowbirds' originated in America where retired RVers head to the southern states during the winter and return to their homelands in the spring. This is a trend increasingly imitated by British RVers who spend the winter months in southern Europe. Even in Australia the "grey nomads" sell up their homes and travel north during the cool months. Like the early camping flocks that overtook the infantile American road network in the beginning of the twentieth century they are dedicated to the nomadic lifestyle and engaged in a continuous pursuit of freedom. The senior RVers' life on the road has become interdependent with the community that is cultivated through clubs and rallies, such as the annual gathering in Quartzite, Arizona where a town the size of about 2,000 people is taken over by more than a million motorhome and caravan enthusiasts. The 'grey age' RVer is a key segment for the motorhome industry and the question is how social and economic changes will fit in with the lifestyle of tomorrow's traveller? In 1950 only eight per cent of the American population was over 60 but by 2040 that figure is expected to rise to more than 20 per cent with Europe and Japan ageing even more rapidly.[23] There is no doubt that the movements and dispositions of this group will have a profound effect on the motorhome industry and culture.

Desert Center, California, USA, February 2001.
Photograph by Jenny Nordquist.

Tin can trash

Meanwhile, the younger generation has found another RV powered pastime. In 2004 the American network Fox dispatched hotel-heiress Paris Hilton and her sidekick Nicole Ritchie on a road trip across America dispossessed of their credit cards and confined to life on the road in an Airstream trailer shared with their miniature dogs. However contrived the plot of this 'surreality' show, the choice of the girls' living quarters is noteworthy. While matching its inhabitants' designer dresses and diamond rings in the style department, the trailer acts as a representation of their downtrodden condition and indicates a latent preconception of the home on wheels going back to the time when it was considered the dwelling for the unlawful outsider.

This notion is also noticeable in our contemptuous attitude toward the permanent mobile home residence. The trailer park is still perceived as the exclusive domicile of 'white trash' while the stigmata of 'trailer trash' has been adapted into language and projected in pop culture by rap artists such as Eminem and his referencing to his Detroit background.[24] Although these reference points are, to an extent, the product of an American cultural identification we have to look no further than British or European shores to find examples of how travel and living on the road is considered the pursuit of the eccentric. The British cabinet minister Margaret Beckett is repeatedly mocked for coming out as caravan enthusiast: "Beckett is the personification of the caravan. She's practical, tough and durable, but rather unexciting and not in the slightest bit glamorous."[25] And when Danish film director Lars von Trier drives his motorhome across Europe to attend the Cannes film festival it is perceived as testament to an unnatural quirkiness never mind the film director's well documented claustrophobia.

However, the prejudices and the connotations we associate with the mobile home are also the product of the RVer's own soul-searching. Throughout history, motorhome enthusiasts have reiterated their affinity with both the gypsy and the pioneer. In 1944 *Motor Caravan* magazine in the UK carried a column called "Down the Lanes with Gypsy Petulengro" (the King of Gypsies) and in the same magazine a series of articles written by the Vagabond of Gloucester were sponsored by a trailer company to promote their postwar caravan model with the tagline: "This life of mine is full of adventure." Dorothy and David Counts note in their anthropological study of RVing seniors in the USA that the contrasting image of the rootless Gypsy and the freedom-seeking pioneer both have their origins in the history of RVing.[26] It's the dichotomy of the identifications that distorts the debate. While the RV community has adapted a romantic aspect of its heritage and culture, the gypsy analogy is often tainted by its use in the political debate over travellers sites, just as the words "mobile home" for some people will trigger the image of a desolate and compromised situation.

Road dreams

The fact is that the mobile home has increasingly become a fashionable and functional alternative for a younger generation of travellers with caravan holidays making up nearly a fifth of all holidays taken in the UK. Newspapers and style magazines routinely feature travel stories addressing an affluent young segment of the population aspiring to the adventurous RV experience rather than bog-standard package holiday, while retro Airstreams and all-inclusive RVs inspire the design-articulate crowd.[27] As the last 100 years have proved, autocamping is an inclusive culture that generates a human interaction across social and economical divide. Six months after my South Dakota RV adventure I spent a week in the Disney-fabricated hyper-reality of Celebration, Florida—an artificially manufactured town presented as a realisation of the American dream for the prosperous. But to me the precision-trimmed grass lawns and white-picket fences constitute a great American illusion. The dream I admire and aspire to flows through gasoline pumps, greasy diners, impromptu boondocking sites and pristine mountain lakes. It is out here that you can trace the noble vagabond's blood vein that runs from the early auto-gypsies to the self-sufficient hippies and surfers who rode the highways and waves fuelled by a yearning for adventure. It is here that you can discover the ingenuity and passion for transposing everyday life to a set of wheels which has fuelled pioneers from Conklin's Gypsy Van to snowbirds who honk their horn and head south when the rest of us sit back and moan. As one London family commented on their decision to travel across Australia in a caravan in 1959: "We rebelled against all the familiar things we resented. We rebelled against convention, security, and the prison of everyday comfort."[28]

Destiny Oasis RV Resort, Las Vegas, USA,
February 2001.
Photograph by Jenny Nordquist.

Endnotes

1. Belasco, Warren James, *Americans on the road: from autocamp to motel, 1910-1945*, MIT Press, 1979, p. 92.

2. Schwantes, Carlos A, *Going Places: transportation redefines the twentieth-century West*, Indiana University Press, 2003, p. 7.

3. Sweeney, M and Davidson J, *On the Move: Transportation and the American Story*, National Geographic Society, 2003, p. 32.

4. Anderson, William C, *The Two-Ton Albatross: Across a trans-continental highway in a travel trailer with two kids, two puppies, a miniature orange tree, a lobster named Hud, a Saint Bernard dog, and a claustrophobic wife*, Crown Publishers, 1969, p. 66.

5. Belasco, *Americans*, p. 24.

6. Cormack, Bill, *A history of holidays 1812-1990*, Routledge, 1998, p. 87.

7. White, Roger B, *Home on the Road: The Motor Home in America*, Smithsonian Books, 2000, p. 26.

8. Belasco, *Americans*, p. 83.

9. Jenkinson, Andrew, *Motorhomes: The Illustrated History*, Veloce Publishing, 2003, p. 15.

10. Belasco, *Americans*, p. 8.

11. Lackey, Kris, *Roadframes: the American Highway Narrative*, University of Nebraska Press, 1997, pp. 5-6.

12. Bedell, Mary Crehore, *Modern Gypsies, The story of a twelve thousand mile motor camping trip encircling the United States*, Williams & Wilkins Co, 1924, p. 262.

13. *The Motor Camper—the official magazine of the Motor Camping Club*, vol 1, no 1, October 1930.

14. *Motor Trailer*, June 1945, p. 117.

15. "A Survey of British Roads", *The Manchester Guardian*, 19 January, 1954, p. 1.

16. Kerr, Joe and Wollen, Peter, eds. *Autopia: cars and culture*, Reaktion, 2002, p. 272.

17. Burkhart, Bryan and Hunt, David, *Airstream: the history of the land yacht*, Chronicle Books, 2000, p. 36.

18. Burkhart and Hunt, *Airstream*, p. 17.

19. White, *Home on the Road*, p. 107.

20. Hutchinson, Roger, *High Sixties: the summer of riot and love*, Mainstream, 1992, p. 63.

21. Perry, Paul, *On the Bus: the complete guide to the legendary trip of Ken Kesey and the Merry Pranksters and the birth of the counterculture*, Thunder's Mouth Press, 1990, p. 112.

22. Townsend, Derek, *Continental Autocamping*, George Allen and Unwin Ltd, 1968, p. 11.

23. Theobald, William F, *Global Tourism*, Butterworth-Heinemann, 2005, p. 512.

24. "He won't have it, he knows his whole back's to these ropes

    It don't matter, he's dope
    He knows that, but he's broke
    He's so stagnant that he knows

    When he goes back to his mobile home,
    That's when it's
    Back to the lab again"

    "Lose Yourself", EMINEM, 2002.

25. White, Roland, "Taking suburbia for a ride out on the open road", *The Sunday Times*, May 8, 2005.

26. Counts, Dorothy Ayers and David R, *Over the next hill: an ethnography of Rving seniors in North America*, Broadview, p. 34.

27. The interior for Airstream's 2000/2001 model was designed by the architect and furniture designer Christopher C Deam.

28. Spear, Diana and George Hammond, *Square Pegs*, Hammond & Company, 1959, p. 9.

Chapter Two

No Place Like Home

Kate Trant

Home comforts

Speaking to motorhome and camper van owners, it is no time at all before the conversation turns to discussing the rewards that for most over-ride the challenging practicalities of living in a home on wheels: independence, freedom and the satisfaction of some kind of pioneering urge. Though the owners in this chapter range from older full-timers in the USA who drive 40 foot motorhomes, to European full and part-timers in both new and classic 'vans, to VW bus owners, for all, taking their home with them gives them the perfect combination: the security and comfort of having with them everything they need, their 'home away from home', and the possibility of going where they like, when they like. In their vehicles, these modern day pioneers, singles, couples, families, groups of friends, are a unit, engaged in something that is both serious and playful. For some, it is almost like playing house, taking a short break from more binding responsibilities, indulging their wanderlust, whilst those who do it for longer periods of time, or even for keeps, are running a home, one on wheels, with particular mechanical challenges and in countries with sometimes unfamiliar rules and regulations. Some desire large horizons and wide open spaces, others are looking for a comfortable change of scenery. Either way, while this lifestyle is not for all, for those it suits, it is a romance — with wide open spaces and with the roads they travel, seeing new things and new places, seeing things from a new perspective.

> *You can take the world in it.*
>
> Sue Johnson talking about the family's camper van, 2005.

While this lifestyle is not for all, for those it suits, it is a romance— with wide open spaces and with the roads they travel, seeing new things and new places, seeing things from a new perspective.

WBCCI Hobo Rally, Blythe, California, February 2001.
Photograph by Jenny Nordquist.

Uncharted territory: freedom and independence

In 1911, an Englishman called Aldred F Barker bought a car that he called 'A.J.' (after its registration number AJ-572) and embarked on a modest motoring tour of the UK. He wrote a book and in 1913, having experienced and understood the freedom offered by the motor-car, he and his wife, Eleanor, set off for a second time in 'A.K.'(AK-367), on a journey around a large proportion of the English and Welsh coastline.[1] This time, instead of relying on hotels, they camped.

> Why turn into an hotel at an unearthly hour in the morning when we might remain out in the open, comfortable and dry amid nature and all her interests and charms?.... The light to the north-east was distinctly brightening, and moonlight was merging into daylight before we put on the side curtains and made ourselves comfortable for a few hours' sleep in the back of the car.... Thus the idea of motor camping first presented itself to us.[2]

These were the early days of a new phenomenon: 'motor-camping' or 'auto-camping'. A variety of types of shelter and sleeping arrangements was set to follow, from tents, to structures that grew out of or were attached to the side of the car, to the development of an interior designed with swivelling seats, "thus making it possible to lie at full length and to pass the night fairly comfortably in the car should necessity demand this."[3]

In mid 1920s America meanwhile, Melville Ferguson's book, *Motor Camping on Western Trails*, aimed to

> ... present in faithful outlines a picture of the every-day routine of a model of travel that is yearly taking a stronger hold upon the fancy of the vacationist who is weary of sticking to conventional ruts and who feels that life owes him a new thrill.
>
> In motor camping there is always adventure round the corner. That is the basis of its widening appeal. If the author shall succeed in persuading the reader who has longingly but hesitatingly contemplated a camping-trip that the price to be paid in discomfort or actual hardship is negligible and the rewards in wholesome and instructive experience rich, his mission will be fulfilled.[4]

In motor camping there is always adventure round the corner.

> **If you go to a place and you don't like it, you can just move somewhere else.**
>
> Sue Johnson.

> **If I don't like it here, all I have to do is turn the key!**
>
> RVing slogan.

Implicit here is the need to satisfy some degree of pioneering spirit, one of the most enduring motivations to be found across all instances of this kind of independent travel.

In neither the USA nor the UK did it take very long for the potential offered by the automobile to be seized by many who recognised its liberating possibilities and motor-camping increased in popularity hugely in the early twentieth century, fulfilling a role as an increasingly economical means of travel whilst also appealing to the wealthier end of the market.

In 1921, Elon Jessup recalls meeting a farmer with his wife and children in Banff:

> ... who were enjoying the marvels of the Canadian Rockies. Their car was a trifle ricketty [sic] in spots but it had brought them safely all the way across the broad Canadian prairies. They had camped out every night and would continue to do so until their return. This farmer explained to me: "I've been wanting to bring my family out and show them this country for years but I couldn't stand the expense till I got the flivver. Going this way don't cost much more than living at home."[5]

I'm at home wherever I choose to park my trailer.

John Culp / USA

John Culp's parents took him tent-camping in the summer of 1926 when he was just nine months old; he remembers the first tent trailer he saw in the early 1930s at a camp ground in Sandusky Ohio.

John does not recall seeing many 'house cars' after the stock market crashed in 1929 and the onset of the Depression in the early 30s. He explains:

> camping and auto-camping faded out for the most part. People had no money, and lots of families lost their homes; tent camps known as 'Hoovervilles' sprung up as their only means of shelter. But by about 1934-35, the 'trailer age' hit and people built 'home-builts' from kits and plans. People could live in these and follow the season, south in winter and north in summer.

"We bought our first 'home-built' in about 1939, built by a local carpenter. We didn't travel with this one, but parked it on a lot in Chippewa Lake and used it like a summer cottage."

In 1945 John's parents bought a used 1942 American and began wintering in Florida and, in 1947, bought the 22 foot Westcraft that he has full-timed in for seven years and still uses today. At $3,200, a thousand dollars more than most contemporary trailers of its size, the Westcraft was considered a luxury.[6]

Then, in 1950, John bought a 1938 Covered Wagon from its original owner which eventually, in 1953, he traded in for a 35 foot Vagabond trailer. He full-timed until 1957 when he married and took up house living. He and his wife, Marge, kept the Westcraft and travelled in it with their son until 1998, when Marge died and John returned to full-timing, travelling with his dog, George, who became something of an RV TV star.

John now spends five months in Florida—his 'headquarters'—five months in Ohio and Michigan and two months on the road.

I'm a holdover from the old trailerite era—true 'trailer trash'—and, in years past, I've been looked down on, discriminated against, had my right to vote questioned, but I would not trade that mobile feeling for the world. It's just great to get on the road in the morning and wonder what's around that next corner and over the next hill.

There's nothing like driving. You get to see what conditions are really like in a place and how people really live. It's the only worthwhile way to travel.

Jim Holifield, "Living the Dream", *The Sacramento Bee*.

Jim and Ginny Holifield / USA

Jim and Ginny Holifield with their 'Lazy Daze' motorhome, complete with map showing the extent of their travels in North and South America.

Jim and Ginny Holifield from Sacramento have had ten motorhomes in the last 45 years, and have driven a total of 1,000,000 miles in that time. They have travelled to every US state, Mexico, Canada, South America, and visited Alaska three times; their three children grew up going on RV trips. It all began when they saw a bus conversion in the 1950s; since then they have converted buses for themselves as well as buying new motorhomes. Their current vehicle is a 26 foot 2002 Lazy Daze. They have been members of the Family Motor Coach Association (FMCA) since 1965, attending every summer convention, and are members of the Good Sam Club.

In 2000, they completed a six month, 23,000 mile trip from Sacramento to Bahia La Pataia, the southern tip of South America and back, a trip that attracted a fair amount of attention. Ginny and Jim and the whole family have been the subject of a range of press articles during their years as RVers, both about their travels and the buses they have converted. In 1970, Jim predicted "motor coaching is the coming thing for family recreation". As *The Sacramento Union* reported: "as he watches his family working out together plans for the bus and trips, he adds: 'It amazes me. But the kids all seem to like this and I can't think of a better hobby.'"[7]

Why should all camper vans be white?

Mag Wakefield / UK

Mag drives a 1984 Bedford CFII Panel Van. She had been looking for a good van at the right price and saw 'Samson' parked at the roadside with a For Sale notice in the windscreen less than five miles from where she lives in Huddersfield. She had spent many happy months driving a Bedford CF ice cream van when she was a student (nearly 30 years earlier) and knew that they had a good reputation mechanically. She bought the van from an art student at Manchester University who could not afford to put it through another MoT; the cost of repairs was slightly more than the price of the van but still reasonable so, according to the log book, Mag became owner number 14. White in 2003, Samson was painted green in 2004.

I had always wanted a camper van and thought I might end up with a VW camper with flowers painted all over it. My partner, Hugh, could never understand what I wanted one for; a few weeks after I had bought Samson, I was still parking him round the corner out of sight, waiting for the right moment to tell Hugh. Then I ran out of petrol so I had to ring him and say something like, "Did I tell you I bought a camper van? I must have forgotten to mention it, and it's run out of petrol, so could you bring me a can?" I think he sees the point now but he can't cope with more than two nights at a time.

Mag takes short breaks in her van, as often as possible, usually within 100 miles of where she lives—Derbyshire Peak District, Lancashire, Cumbria and the Lake District. She and Hugh stay on small campsites, pubs and farms and sometimes wildcamp; they avoid big sites unless they have absolutely no alternative. She also visits France through *France Passion*, a scheme through which French farmers and producers allow 'camping-caristes' free overnight stays on their land. The scheme works on the recognition that the visitors are likely to buy the farm produce during their stay.

You can stay overnight in amazing places and wake up in the morning surrounded by fantastic views and fresh, unpolluted air. Then you can go for a long walk, or set off in the van and cruise along to find another spot to stop. Zero stress, no timetable, a minimum of technology and, ideally, no neighbours.

Festivals are part of what we do—we go in the van.

Amanda Pearson and Peter Dunnet / UK

Amanda and Peter bought their long wheelbase Mercedes 508D in the summer of 1998. A C-reg, 'Foxy' was 20 years old in 2005. They bought it via LOOT, London's 'free ads' newspaper through which many Londoners buy and sell.

Long-term festival-goers, the couple had seen many Mercedes vans and, having decided they wanted a motorhome, started their search. They looked at a variety of vehicles, even considering buying a vehicle and paying someone to turn it into a motorhome for them, but eventually they bought a van from someone on the other side of London, and Peter set about converting it for the two of them. "For a whole year, a VW was too small and an RV was out of our price bracket."

Both Amanda and Peter had for a while held a fantasy of moving out of London and the two planned the journey that was to take them all round Europe for more or less a year. Part of the travel involved 'Willing Workers in Organic Farms'—they wanted to see how commercially viable organic farming might be and whether they could make a living this way on their return to the UK.

> It's very, very hard to break away from the rat-race existence. It was about five years between starting the conversations about changing our lives and actually doing it. We changed our lives temporarily for a year; ultimately we want to change our lives completely.

They set sail from Newcastle to Amsterdam on 21 March 1999; neither of the pair are sun-seekers so they travelled round Northern Europe in the summer and Southern Europe in the winter. They combined touring and sightseeing with working on organic farms and kept in constant contact by email with friends at home, who fed them information and ideas.

One of the great advantages of converting the van themselves was that Peter could fit it out according to their needs.

> We had conversations about what we needed. One important thing is that we have always tried to have an open fire. Ways of keeping warm are important to us, more important that showers and toilets. So we have a wood burning stove in the van.

You are limited by space but it's amazing how little you do actually need.

They discovered that organic farming as a commercial enterprise was not for them; since their return, they have settled—for the timebeing at least—in Wales.

*Amanda Pearson and Peter Dunnet's
Mercedes 508D.*

Home away from Home The World of Camper Vans and Motorhomes

Contemporary tin can tourists

The Tin Can Tourists, an organisation founded in 1919 and which flourished throughout the 1930s, went into a decline at the end of the decade and, in this incarnation, ceased to exist by the mid 1970s. In 1998, Forrest and Jeri Bone revived the club.

Top: Forrest and Jeri Bone's 1958 Spartan.

Bottom: Forrest and Jeri Bone's 1949 Spartanette Model 24.

You meet the nicest people at vintage rallies and gatherings.

Forrest and Jeri Bone / USA

Forrest and Jeri Bone's vintage trailers include a 1949 Spartanette Model 24, a 1950 American, a 1957 Buckeye, a 1958 Spartan and a 1963 Avion. They first joined the Vintage Airstream Club and then became interested in all makes and models, renewing the Tin Can Tourists in 1998.

Forrest explains:

> The Tin Can Tourists were organised in 1919 in Tampa, Florida and grew to over 100,000 members in the 1930s. Winter Conventions were held in Arcadia and Sarasota, as well as Tampa. A summer reunion was held in the Midwest, mostly in Traverse City, Michigan. The travel trailer boom began to recede in the late 1930s—the war and then a shift to the production of larger mobile homes to accommodate the needs of returning military personnel put the club into membership decline. My wife and I renewed the group in 1998 as an all-make and model vintage trailer and motor coach club. We have seen the group build steadily over the past seven years. Our renewal gathering in 1998 attracted 21 trailers; there were 115 vintage RVs at the most recent rally and 240 people came to dinner on the Saturday night.

Forrest and Jeri travel to the Florida Keys each year, as well as to Tin Can Tourist rallies. They enjoy the freedom this lifestyle offers and the interest it generates in others; if they could add any vehicle they wanted to their collection, they would choose a Covered Wagon from the 1930s.

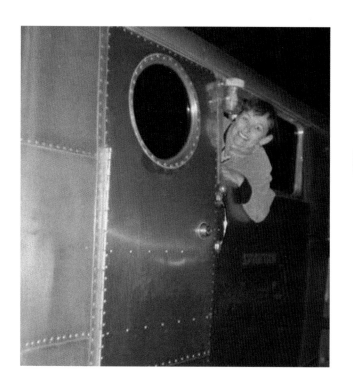

My trailercoach is not a home away from home, it is my home.

Mai Billaud / USA

Tin Can Tourist Mai Billaud lives in her 1949 Spartan Royal Mansion. A retired art curator, she acquired "this marvellous gem in engineering and craftsmanship" almost two years ago and, though she did not plan to live in it initially, she has done ever since.

Mai Billaud's 1949 Spartan Royal Mansion.

For one night only

The 1978 VW Campmobile...

Commer

Auto-Sleeper

The satisfaction of the desire for freedom and independence depends to a large extent on the nature of the overnight stays that are possible. Whilst a great deal of marketing material emphasises the lonely, wide open spaces available for the night, with vehicles parked in exquisite isolation and couples gazing wistfully into the distance, the contemporary reality can be somewhat different. Over time, the increasing organisation of campsites and camping activities in general has dictated that overnight stays, long and short, have become an increasingly structured activity. Initially this came about in part because of the suspicion that was attached to travelling people, temporary living and the nomadic existence and, as it increased, in many cases so did the desire for unstructured living. Today, some turn a blind eye to these 'structures' and continue to get from motorhome and camper ownership what they need; other owners are happy to arrive at a campsite destination for a night or more and take advantage of the facilities that are offered. 'Hooking up' inevitably imposes some kind of order as, by necessity, vehicles must drive up to fixed utilities—water, power and waste; in some campsites, owners can even drive their vehicle into an existing plot of land, a ready-made garden. At some US sites, formal and informal, it is more or less accepted that long-term, regular, repeat visitors have their own 'spot' to return to each time.

Today, the least structured end of the spectrum in the USA is 'boondocking' or, in the UK, 'wildcamping'. The term 'boondocking' comes from the expression "living in the boonies", and means living with no need for external support water, waste, power, etc.. Many contemporary motorhomes are fully equipped with facilities that enable owners to stay in one place for periods of up to two weeks and more without the need to use external utility supplies. For many, this is a key requirement when selecting their vehicle; if they have no intention to boondock or wildcamp, the choice of vehicle can be very different. For some, boondocking is a practicality based on financial necessity; for others it is more of an attitude and a way of life. Meanwhile there are many who boondock some of the time, and use campsites when required.

For many RVers, freedom is equated with boondocking. Boondockers are free to go where they want when they want, and to leave on a moment's notice if they choose. While those who prefer formal parks may claim the same enjoyment of and commitment to freedom, many boondockers disagree. They maintain that a park-oriented RVing style requires advance planning, an inflexible schedule and reservations for each night.[8]

Today, boondocking in the USA is still a more viable proposition than wildcamping in the UK and Europe. In addition, there is less of a culture in the UK and Europe for independent overnight stays. As much as anything, this is historical; the pioneering spirit that comes from the need to travel huge distances is more deeply embedded in US RVing than in European motorhome use. Meanwhile, security remains a concern for some choosing an overnight site.

In the USA, RVers are able to use WalMart car parks as their stopover points; as a result, most of those stopping use the supermarkets for their shopping. An owner explains: "I have just returned from a 13,500 mile trip from the Mexican border at San Diego to the Arctic Circle in Alaska. In all that time we used parking sites of WalMart as our night time stopover points."[9]

In the UK, motorhome owners feel less well catered for and compare the situation in the UK unfavourably with other European countries, particularly France, where the network of 'aires de service' allows overnight stays. 'Stopovers UK' is a campaign launched by *Motor Caravan Magazine* that challenges the attitude towards overnight camping in Britain, aiming to encourage local authorities to provide areas for short-term overnight stays.[10] A lively debate continues amongst owners and in the pages of the motor caravanning press.

Some like to carefully plan their journey, others relish the unknown. For them, the journey is a means to an end, not the end it itself.

> Some people never have a destination…. The road calls them, and they find it hard to stay in one place more than a few days. They revel in the freedom to go where they want, stay as long as they please, and leave when they get the urge.[12]

Dormobile opens new frontiers

Top: Dormobile marketing brochure.
Collection of Malcolm Bobbitt.

Opposite: Nevada, USA, February 2001.
Photograph by Jenny Nordquist.

Top of the road, left or right?

Gaynor and Graham Stevens / UK

Gaynor, an accountant, and her husband Graham, who is a mechanic, drive a Sun Sport around the UK and Europe. They have had a number of different vehicles ranging from their first Transit, followed by a Bedford Pioneer, then a 28 foot Eldorado. Though they are not full-timers, they travel all year round—Graham races on the Autograss circuit and the couple use their motorhome to go to meetings. They have had the Sun Sport for nearly two years and are thinking about getting something bigger again, maybe 30 feet.

"The first one was a Transit; that was amazing because it had a cooker and a fridge and everything in it, but it was mini-bus sized." Deciding they needed something bigger, they bought the Pioneer. "Then we saw the American ones and thought, price-wise, you're not going to beat that in value." Gaynor feels that 'Americans' are about style, size and quality, and the way that the interior space is used successfully. "They really know how to build them." Many owners of American motorhomes comment on the benefits of having a fixed bed, rather than one that has to be brought out and put away in order to use space properly.

> With a 'European' you 'drop the bench down here, move this seat' to get a bed which is not very comfortable anyway. But with these you've got a fixed bed, which is a benefit because, when you park up somewhere, it could be the middle of the night and you can't see what you're doing.

> Because it's got central heating we use this right through the winter. It's instant heat. There's a gas boiler which is run by a thermostat, which is lovely, because you can lie in bed in the morning, switch it on, the boiler lights and all these air vents blow out hot air. There's one in the loo as well which is rather nice.

Their motorhome has an on-board generator meaning that they are self-contained and can camp anywhere they choose, though they have yet to do any wildcamping.

"We do go to camps. In France camping is so cheap anyway. You can camp on a site with all mod cons, and you are paying something like £5 or £6 a night."

It's about freedom.

The key is that travelling in a motorhome, RV or camper offers a range of possible lifestyles; though there are common themes and similar approaches, there is a whole spectrum of types of people and reasons for doing it and there are as many ways of living life in a home on wheels as there are people who live it.[12]

Many motorhome owners identify the feeling of community that they encounter on their travels as being one of the reasons for continuing: "It is the quest for freedom and independence that lures elderly people into RVing life on the road, but, paradoxically, it is the communities they find and build there that keep them travelling for years."[13]

Gaynor and Graham Stevens' Sun Sport.

If you're on a campsite and you lift up the bonnet, before you know it, you're surrounded by offers of help.

Terry and Sue Martin / UK

Terry and Sue Martin first had a boat that they kept on the Thames. A four-berth cabin cruiser, they would use it for weekends and holidays cruising up and down the river. For them, boat and motorhome lifestyles are similar. On a practical level, many activities are held in common, including the need to bring on board fresh water and other supplies. "But with the boat, we always had to think about getting to it. With a motorhome, we don't have that problem. It's always parked in the drive. It's more flexible too; we use it all the year round." A social dimension is familiar to both too and the couple have met a great number of friends through both their boat and motorhome use.

Their first motorhome was a 1983 Pioneer 1004. At first they travelled in the UK but then started to travel further afield, to France, Germany, Holland and Luxembourg. Since the Pioneer, they had a number of Europeans, then a Mallard Sprinter imported from the USA. "A friend had bought an American and we liked the quality and the facilities, like power steering and cruise control. Everything you could think of was there."

A second American, a 23 foot Sun Sport 6.2 diesel followed in 1993 then, in 1998, the couple returned to a European, a 2.5 diesel Swift Lifestyle. Until then they had had a dog which meant that they needed more room; she died and they decided to go to something smaller. "Layout-wise it was very good and Europeans do better mileage to the gallon. But I was always trying to put my foot through the floor to make it go quicker."

They joined The Motor Caravanners' Club in 1982. "We were most impressed by the groups that hold meets in places that you wouldn't normally go to."

You explore places because you have got the time. It opens up the whole country.

Top: Terry and Sue's first van, a Bedford Pioneer 1004, 1983.

Bottom: Their second van, a CRU Dreamliner, 1984.

... and their fifth van, a Gulfstream Sun Sport 6.2D Chevrolet.

Free to go

Here's to a whole new chapter.

About Schmidt

Winnebago Adventurer.
Courtesy of Winnebago Industries, Inc.

RVers assert that houseguests and fish stink after three days— they're right.

Dorothy and David Counts / USA

Early in the 1990s, two Canadian anthropologists, Dorothy and David Counts, embarked on a major study of RVing seniors in North America. Not only did they publish the results in *Over the Next Hill*, inspired by what they encountered, they bought their own 23 foot fifth wheel trailer, a 2000 Kit Corp Espre towed by a 1998 Dodge diesel truck, which they use to tour the USA and Canada visiting friends and family.[14] Meanwhile the book is in its second edition. The couple has also worked with the Recreation Vehicle Industry Association (RVIA), giving lectures and interviews on the phenomenon of full-time RVing.

Their love of RVing first came about because of a chance meeting with some 'full-timers' in 1978 which, in turn, lead them to embark on their study. They bought their current vehicle second hand and, though no restoration work was needed, they modified it considerably by, for example, re-designing shelving and storage to create more usable space. Trips in their RV range from weekend visits to the homes of relatives who live close by, to six to eight week cross-continental journeys. In 2005, they spent six weeks travelling 6,000 miles to visit three of their children—in British Columbia and Ontario.

They have been struck by one significant change in the world of RVing since their first involvement: the increase in the size of rigs.

> When we first did our research in 1993/94, we had a 30 foot pull trailer, without a slide, that we pulled with an old van. Now we frequently see rigs that are 40 foot long with three slideouts, that are so heavy that they have to be pulled by a medium duty truck and are too long and wide to fit into the parking spaces in many of the older parks. We don't even want to think about the fuel budget for them...

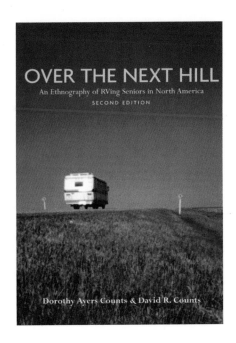

Top: Over the Next Hill, Dorothy and David Counts' book presenting the findings of their major study of RVing seniors in North America.

Bottom: Fleetwood Pace Arrow, 2005.

Jack calls it the highlight of our twilight.

Meet the Fockers

The culture of RVing in North America is firmly established and widespread, with large organisations representing both industry and owner. Today, a record 7.2 million RVs are on US roads and the RV industry in the USA is worth over $14 billion a year, the term "RV" was the number one search term on the increasingly significant cultural barometer, eBay, in 2004 and nearly one in 12 US vehicle-owning households—nearly seven million households—now owns an RV.

> As the population has aged toward retirement, the No. 1 [eBay] search term has shifted from Gucci (2002) and BMW (2003) to this year's leading term, RV, short for recreational vehicle. The kind you buy when you sell the house and tour Florida campgrounds in a Winnebago.[15]

Although the market is changing, the largest proportion of RVers in the USA and Canada belong to the 'grey generation'. However, though the figures for the total number of RVers are not absolute they support the dominant image of the RVer as older, retired or semi-retired, either single or part of a couple, full or part-timing.[16]

The numbers in the UK are equally difficult to pin down though it is likely that in 2004, new purchases of motorhomes were in the region of 8,000, while 30,000 second-hand motorhomes changed hands. In the UK and North America, owners are both full and part-time. Some sell their homes and commit permanently to a nomadic lifestyle, while those in a financial position to do so keep their homes and travel to warmer climes for the winter months while others rent their homes out in order to do the same; many use their motorhomes for holidays and weekend breaks. On both sides of the Atlantic, owners drive a whole host of different vehicles, from the huge Fleetwood seen in *Meet the Fockers*— a "custom-designed, climate-controlled motorcoach that is bigger than our apartment", to the often only slightly smaller Europeans driven in the UK and elsewhere.[17] Both also have a large and active classic vehicle circuit, amongst which are found very many cherished older vehicles that have survived the ravages of time and travel. Some vehicles cross from one side of the Atlantic to the other, predominantly west to east, from the USA to the UK, though the ubiquitous VW bus has made its presence felt across continents.

We can sleep in our own beds, eat our own food, use our own bathroom without stopping at every other gas station, and take our dogs with us.

Jim Brightly / USA

Jim Brightly, Technical Editor of the *Family Motor Coaching* magazine, drives a 1999 25 foot Type A Allegro motorhome; he and his wife are currently replacing all the furniture, wallpaper and floor coverings. Both are keen off-roaders and graduated to a motorhome from camping in a tent, via a tent trailer and a camper. They visit their children and grandchildren 200 miles away in Southern California, and then travel with them to the desert and mountains where they camp and drive their Jeeps on the local trails.

The freedom and flexibility to go wherever, whenever.

Lynn Lamon and Linda Walden / USA

Lynn and Linda, from West Carrollton in Ohio, drive a 40 foot 2000 American Dream diesel pusher motorhome. They shopped carefully, including going to the FMCA International Convention in Iowa in August 1999 to look at comparable brands and models, and eventually bought it, new, in October the same year.

The couple love to travel and, after living in Hawaii for eight years, decided to return to the mainland and try their hand at full-time RVing. The first night they spent as full-timers, in a new 24 foot Class C Fleetwood Jamboree

Searcher, was the first night they had ever spent in an RV. After a year of full-timing, they traded to a 35 foot Class A Fleetwood Southwind which they travelled in for two years, and then traded up to their current motorhome. They generally move to a different park every two weeks using membership RV parks with two-week stay restrictions.

Lynn and Linda retired early, at 39 and 37, and moved to the Caribbean where they taught scuba-diving, then onto Hawaii, where they developed a business using their diving skills and shooting and teaching underwater photography and video. Their experience and knowledge led to them writing and producing photographs for a diving magazine and it is these skills that, once they began RVing, led them to write for *Motor Home* and *Highways*, two US RVing publications.

Lynn and Linda are very closely involved in their RVing community. They are 'Escapees' (SKPs), members of the Escapee Boomer BoF (Birds of a Feather)—a group within the Escapee RV Club that caters for the 'Baby Boomer' generation of RVers, and members of the FMCA. They are active in the FMCA Chapter called "Habitat for Humanity"; Linda is President, while Lynn is National Director.

We love full-timing and have no plans to do anything else.

... spending time with other RVers talking, playing cards and dominoes, cooking and eating.

Sam and Shirley Gallo / USA

Sam Gallo and his wife Shirley, from Louisiana, travel in a 34 foot 2003 Holiday Rambler which they use for regular short trips in Louisiana and longer trips further afield about six times a year. They are also members of the Holiday Rambler RV Club, a club started in 1964 specifically for Holiday Rambler owners with its own magazine, *Ramblings*, the FMCA and the Good Sam Club, taking part in rallies and "spending time with other RVers talking, playing cards and dominoes, cooking and eating".

Top: Sam and Shirley Gallo with their
Holiday Rambler.

Bottom: A gathering of the Acadiana Ramblers.

Overleaf: Quartzsite, Arizona, USA, 2001.
Photograph by Jenny Nordquist.

Flying south for the winter

For eight months of the year, Quartzsite in Arizona is empty. From November onwards each year however, 175,000 RVs (over 1 million people) fill 79 trailer parks and front yards, and seven miles either side of town. The majority are dry camping or boondocking—that is the vehicles are self-contained and need only the occasional hookups to take out waste and take on water. They are 'snowbirds', elderly Americans and Canadians who follow the sun, travelling south to warmer weather for the winter.[18]

There are 'snowbirds' in Europe too, with motorhome owners swelling the ranks of retired homeowners in southern Spain. As in North America, owners often have a home in the UK as well as a motorhome or rent their homes and travel for the winter. Some sell up their UK homes and commit to full-timing. Many drive south from the UK in winter, coming back for the warmer summer months, meeting up at the major motorhome shows that take place in the UK throughout the summer to swap stories and catch up with one another. The 'season' opens with what is known as 'Peterborough', the National Motorhome Show, that takes place each April, and closes with 'Shepton Mallett' in September after which they leave for the sun, boarding ferries for Spain, France, Portugal and Italy.

Long Beach, Los Angeles, USA, February 2001.
Photograph by Jenny Nordquist.

You haven't had the full RV experience until you've been to Quartzsite in January.

Phyllis Frey, "America's Largest Parking Lot", National Geographic.

Excess baggage

One of the myths associated with the full-time RVing and motorhome lifestyle is that those who are doing it are wilfully 'spending their children's inheritance' and, as Dorothy and David Counts explain,

> their choice is also seen as one inappropriately separating them from children and grandchildren. At the time of their lives when they should be surrounded by their children and dandling their grandchildren on their knees, they are off partying in the desert.[19]

The reality is that many do exactly the opposite, settling their affairs and distributing their belongings amongst their children before they make the break to full-timing, and making the most of their mobile lifestyle by visiting their children and grandchildren more than they might do if they lived a more static way of life. Many owners feel that their visits are more satisfactory because they can remain independent of their families for the duration. Many owners live by a rule of thumb common to those living in a small space of any sort: on buying something new, an existing possession has to go.

They talk about 'motorhome mellow'. A lot of the stress of life tends to disappear.

You can only ever be in one room at a time, can't you?

Glo and Col / UK

Glo and Col have been full-timing in an American for 15 months, regularly travelling 40 miles a day around the UK. Publicans for most of their careers, their last house was a six-bedroom B&B. "We've only ever lived in 'big'; but in the 15 months we've had this, I've never felt hemmed in."

Glo used to collect 'things': "I was the biggest hoarder in the world, a collector; I gave the collections to the kids."

When Glo became ill, her priorities changed significantly and both she and Col began to think that travelling would be ideal. Originally not planning to buy an American, they saw a range at the Stratford show in October 2003. "When we left Stratford we knew we didn't want a European. In Europeans you have to fiddle about with the bed. In an American, the bed is always made. And the layout works; it's so airy."

In January 2004, they sold their house and have been on the road ever since, wildcamping and using campsite facilities at least once a week. Their motorhome has everything that they need: "That's my conservatory, that's my lounge, that's my dining room..." and both became National Trust and English Heritage members—"that's our garden."

We're still learning; we learn something new more or less every day.

Their attitude to life has changed significantly since going full-time. They plan about a month ahead, depending on what they need to be doing: "They talk about 'motorhome mellow'. A lot of the stress of life tends to disappear."

The kids think we're wonderful; they think we're following our dream. The grandchildren think we're cool. They come and stay; they always want to stay.

Glo and Col's *Four Winds 5000* at the National Motorhome Show 2005 in Peterborough.

American dreams

A handful of businesses and individuals in the UK import huge US motorhomes—Americans—for owners who want a home with bigger and better facilities and space. These range from individuals who travel to the USA, buy a vehicle, travel in it for a year or so, then import it to the UK where they sell it and go off and do it all over again, to businesses set up to import US vehicles.

One of the key differences between a European and American motorhome is the 'slide-out', a way to add internal space by winding out additional sections to the main body of the vehicle, on hydraulics, when it is stationary. Many American motorhomes have slide-outs; Europeans do not—at least for the moment.

Top and bottom: typical slide-out arrangement adding space to an 'American' motorhome when stationary.
Courtesy National RV.

A European is a stage up from camping; an American is really a home away from home.

Jane and Mark, Porsche and Morgan Edwards / UK / USA

Jane and Mark Edwards run Destination RV International, a company based in the west of England that imports into the UK a range of American motorhomes to meet an increasing demand for these larger vehicles. Spending six months of the year in the USA and six months in the UK, they find and import both new and pre-owned vehicles.

> I look at the interiors, Mark looks at the engineering. We have people in the USA who have looked for us over the years. So, if we are asked for something specific we'll ask them to look for it. We usually narrow it down to mileage and price, and go and look at it ourselves. Then we ship them over to the UK; it can take eight weeks, maybe longer.

Before their first motorhome, Jane and Mark were surfers and had converted their own van into a motorhome. They also kept a boat.

> It was costing us a fortune in marina fees and we realised that we might just as well stand at the end of the pontoon and throw in £3,000 a year. We decided that with a motorhome at least you could use it in all weathers, not just when it was a nice day. And it was more versatile. So we bought our first American. We refurbished it—Mark did it up and I did the interiors, then we sold it.

The couple began to build a reputation for their knowledge of American motorhomes and prospective buyers would ask them to view possible purchases with them. In 1996, they went into business full-time.

Jane and Mark's young son, Morgan, already looks after the vehicles with his parents. He remembers travelling to France regularly in the family's first motorhome, a Leprechaun Coachmen, and is as passionate about American motorhomes as his parents, referring to Europeans as "the MFIs". He spends his summers touring the shows with his parents and says, "I'll be selling them when I'm older."

His older sister Porsche meanwhile, remembers the same holidays in France. "The more we went, the more we wanted to do. On the way we would sleep, dance, draw and jump on the bed. Everything was exciting and it felt like home."

Every day was different whereas when we were at home, every day was the same.

Both children have travelled extensively and are now home-schooled.

I'd been to the US once before when I was two. When we are there now we live in an RV and tour round looking for RVs. I've been to places including Florida, Georgia, Tennessee, Kentucky and Key West. I like the US; when I'm here I miss things over there but it's the same the other way round.

Jane's perception of the reasons people travel in motorhomes is based on a great deal of experience in dealing with different buyers:

People buy motorhomes because they are happier in their own environment. If you go to a hotel, you can't take your animals, you have to stay in one place, you have to get up and go down to breakfast before, say, eight o'clock. A lot of people don't want that. But, at the same time, they still want the luxury and comfort that being at home will offer them. It's a bit like being

a tortoise—you can take it with you. You have still got those home comforts, but you can travel at the same time. I know in a European motorhome you have still got some of those comforts but there is no comparison between a 'European' and an 'American'. Although you've got the fridge/freezers, you can only get in a small packet of peas.

Jane is interested in the development of motorhome design, recognising that, as with the development of the car itself, the basic configuration of the motorhome was established very early on in its development and that, almost a century on, modifications remain very slight and within a relatively small range of options. Interior layouts revolve around the placing of the beds, the relative positions of the sleeping, cooking, eating and sitting areas, all within the constraints of limited space. Even the apparently recent introduction of superdecks—external decks—on contemporary motorhomes can be found in early twentieth century vehicles.

Jane and Mark are very aware of the differences both between the USA and Europe, but also between the UK and the rest of Europe.

We have travelled a lot of the west coast of France where they are more advanced than we are in this country in terms of dealing with motorhomes. They want people to go there. They set up car parks next door to the beaches and the sea-front so that motorhomes can park, because they know that if you're there, you're spending money. Whereas, in the UK, we don't. We put up height restrictors, and "No overnight camping" signs; then people have to move off into the wild where there's nothing they can spend their money on.

For UK owners, buying a pre-owned American is not impossible—especially during periods with beneficial exchange rates. A second hand vehicle can cost the same as a European at the top end of the market. For Jane and Mark, the choice is clear: "You can buy an American for the same sort of money, with a better chassis, glass windows, big fridge/freezers, fixed beds, air conditioning units, central heating—so why go for one of those when you can have one of these?"

… why go for one of those when you can have one of these?

Euro visions

The 1950s and 1960s in the UK saw a whole host of vehicles that are rarely seen on the roads today though members of clubs like the Classic Camper Club maintain a range of pre-1985 vehicles, while The Motor Caravanners' Club is the only one in the UK catering solely for motorcaravans. Growing out of the Camping and Caravan Club, it now has around 12,500 members. Vehicles can be any size and any age.

> ## Start off with the premise that fitting your life into an elongated box means compromise. You make mistakes, move on and get something else.

Rick and June Whittaker / UK

Rick and June Whittaker have been motor caravanning since the mid 1990s. They became members of The Motor Caravanners' Club in 1995/96 after some friends invited them to join. Founded in 1960, the Club came about for a very particular reason; Rick explains the early days:

> The motivation for the first Motor Caravanners' Club members was 'self-build'. These people were working families, parents with limited disposable income. With the increasing popularity of motorhomes in the UK, self-build developed because it was the way to have a cheap, economical motor caravan. Motor caravanners are different to caravanners and tenters and they forged their own alliance: The Motor Caravanners' Club.

Rick has had a number of different vehicles, including two VW buses, an Auto-sleepers Clubman because, though not particularly cheap to run, it was "the prettiest little van on the market", four Hymers and now a Niesmann + Bischoff.

> The way to choose your motorhome is to find the best layout for you. Start off with the premise that fitting your life into an elongated box means compromise. You make mistakes, move on and get something else. It's almost impossible to get it right the first time but the saving grace is that the depreciation on these vehicles is not as painful as it is on some.

> ## The reason there are so many failed self-built projects is that, when you start a home built project, it rapidly becomes apparent what a heck of a project it is; people start and then never finish.

Although there are some very expensive rigs around, you don't have to be wealthy to own a motorhome or camper; if they're roadworthy and cheap, they are just as enjoyable.

Martin Watts / UK

Martin Watts was founder of the Classic Camper Club in 1991. He bought this Ford Transit ERF Roadranger (registered in 1974) from a Club member three years ago. Only 200 or so were ever built, and few have survived, so he jumped at the chance to buy this one. He paid a little over £1,000 for it, with an MOT, though it did require running repairs (and still does). He also has a 1967 Commer Car-Camper that he bought from a doctor in the Midlands in 1992; although it was apparently in excellent order when he bought it, the rear spring hangers collapsed a year later and the rear end (underneath) had to be completely rebuilt. It was used for family holidays both in the UK and trips to France, for many years and has had many thousands spent on it. Now unused for about four years, Martin's 15 year old son (who adores the van) is restoring it in his spare time.

Martin first became interested in the world of motorcaravans through his parents. The family spent a couple of weeks touring France and Holland in the late 1960s in a converted ambulance. His father later converted a mobile butcher's van into a camper before buying a 1964 Commer Caravan in the late 60s.

"I believe that it really is a 'love it or loathe it' type of hobby. Experience has taught me that many children brought up by motor-homing parents often buy one themselves in later years."

Martin uses his van for weekend trips, club rallies, classic vehicle displays and holidays: two overseas trips with the Classic Camper Club, one to France and one to Holland plus independent family holidays to France and around the UK. He is also a familiar sight in the pages of a range of motorhoming magazines.

Every journey is an adventure in an older model—wondering if you will reach your destination without the aid of a tow-truck!

It really is a case of, have kitchen and bed, will travel! Complete freedom and independence from the stresses and strains of twenty-first century life.

If Martin could have any motorhome of his choice, he would choose

without doubt a classic American Airstream motorhome from the 1970s. Pure heaven! It just has to be the sexiest motorhome ever built, and never bettered to this day. My second choice would be the model that I already own, a Ford Transit ERF Roadranger. I wanted one when I first saw one years ago, and my dream came true!

Martin Watts' Ford Transit ERF Roadranger.

If you have ever wanted to meander gently through the countryside, visit local art galleries or museums, wander through the quiet country roads, walk on deserted beaches and enjoy the fresh air—in comfort, then a motorhome is for you. They are fun and offer complete freedom and flexibility. They are terrific for singles, honeymooners, families, retirees and everyone in between.

Tony Wilson, www.motorhomesworldwide.com

Tony Wilson / Australia

Tony Wilson has a long pedigree in the world of motorhomes and camper vans. Now based in Australia, where he emigrated in the early 1970s, he and his family have been involved in the automotive industry for 100 years in the UK and, increasingly, around the world. His grandfather and grandmother ran the first driving school in the UK, and set up a car dealership in the early years of the twentieth century.

> The story really started when my grandfather, Howard Wilson, who was a fish and poultry merchant, had a good year and decided to buy one of the new cars that were just beginning to appear on the roads of the UK. He spoke to a Mr Herbert Austin and was soon driving around the area. A friend of his admired the car so Howard Wilson told Herbert Austin and, shortly thereafter, his friend came round to show off his new car. A few days later a cheque for 'introductory commission' arrived in the mail from Herbert Austin! Howard thought this was great and, in 1904, he started Wilsons Automobiles & Coachworks Ltd.

Wilsons Motor Caravan Centre started in 1958, and was the largest global motorhome dealership throughout the 1960s and 1970s, selling over 2,000 motorhomes each year and supplying motorhomes to many celebrities including Steve McQueen and Graham Hill. Now Tony's agency, Motorhomes Worldwide, offers a vast range of motorhomes and camper vans to rent, in a similarly large range of countries.

Advertisement in Autocar, 14 October 1966.
Collection of Robin Hudson.

You can pull up and have a nice cup of tea whenever you feel like it.

Keith and Hilary Schofield / UK

Keith and Hilary Schofield have a 1971 Commer Tourstar and a Burstner 748-2 Motorhome. "We feel that we have the best two motor caravans at the moment: the Classic for the vast interest shown in her by likeminded people, and the Burstner for long haul and European travel." They bought the Commer Tourstar in 1998 and restored the exterior; the interior is original. They travel in it, covering 1,000 miles around Scotland in seven days recently, and take it to shows and rallies too.

Keith Schofield with the first owners of their Commer Tourstar, Mr Eric and Mrs Kathleen Stables in 1998.

You have the independence to go or stay wherever you please, you always have your own home comforts with you and, when you get to your destination, you know where you are going to sleep.

A motor caravan gives you the best of all worlds. It's home from home wherever you go.

Bob and Joyce Nicholson / UK

Bob and Joyce Nicholson, from Scotland, use their 1991 Swift Kontiki for all their leisure time, whether at weekends or a few weeks away, and always for holidays. Now that they are both retired, they can spend a lot more time travelling and are able to do journeys in more leisurely stages. Bob was a motor mechanic, and interested in camping, "so it was an almost natural progression into motor caravans which combined both my interests". Members of both the Classic Camper Club and the Camping and Caravanning Club, they spend some of their time at rallies and shows and, in May 2005, they organised Skye's the Limit, a two week trip in Scotland for 24 vans from the Classic Camper Club.

Bob and Joyce Nicholson in Cherbourg, 2004.

It drives like a car, gives you the freedom to explore and enjoy so many places, and gives you the independence no other type of vehicle does.

We are mainly interested in old vans of the 50s and 60s but we don't ignore modern vans and campers.

Steve Pepper / UK

The International Register of Microcaravans was started in 1997 in the UK by enthusiast Steve Pepper because of the lack of information he could find on the smaller vans that were in their heydey in the 1950s and early 60s. The Fiat Amigo and the Honda Romahome are examples of these diminutive versions of mobile living.

I was at a National Microcar Rally and had just bought a 1960s Raleigh folding caravan to tow behind my mini-engined, three-wheeled Berkeley T60 microcar. A fellow microcar owner more or less challenged me to form a club for microcaravans, and eight years and 34 issues of *Micro Caravan News* later, The International Register of Microcaravans is still going strong. We are mainly interested in old vans of the 50s and 60s but we don't ignore modern vans and campers and have done reviews of the Pod, T@B and the recently-launched Sleeper from Falcon Cars, which weighs in at under 1 cwt and can be towed by a bubble car.

We are literally international with members as far afield as Canada, Turkey and Australia; we all live too far apart to have our own rally but I see many of them at the various microcar rallies throughout the year.

Steve has a Bedford Bambi Motor Caravan and a 1955 Berkeley Caravette.

Steve Pepper with his Bedford Bambi Motor Caravan.

Roll your own

Make your truck groovy, and you will feel groovy in your truck!

Roll Your Own.

In 1964, when Ken Kesey and the Merry Pranksters were travelling from California to New York to see the World's Fair in a converted 1939 International Harvester school bus called "Further", the VW bus was being marketed as a versatile business vehicle as well as becoming the icon of surf culture and a whole host of European motorhomes were being marketed as clean-cut, economical ways to see the ever-widening horizons of Europe. At one and the same time, the mobile lifestyle was a hippy, non-conformist, counter-cultural alternative and a version of middle class suburban life in miniature.

Roll Your Own, 1974's guide to alternative living.
Collection of Sam Worthington.

Some things, it's nice to see, just never change. The VW bus stood apart from the crowd when the children of the Sixties were dropping out, and it's still a vehicle for the alternative-minded now that they've dropped back in. Of course, these days the VW bus's special attractiveness results from engineering refinement rather than countercultural appeal. But in our studied opinion, there's still only one way to describe it: far out, man, really far out.

"Volkswagen Vanagon", *Car and Driver*, February 1980.

Top: Volkswagen Micro Bus marketing
brochure, 1957.
Collection of Everett Barnes.

Bottom: Aussie Surf Wagon at Greg Noll's
Surf Shop, Hermosa Beach, 1965,
by LeRoy Grannis.
Courtesy of LeRoy Grannis.

In 1974, *Roll Your Own*[20] suggested that:

The top half of a VW bus, or 'bug', sliced off and welded onto the roof of your rig, is another popular possibility for added space and light to your living quarters. You'll need welding tools, time, know-how and determination to do as extensive an addition as this.

Friends of ours bought an old VW bus body in Wisconsin for ten dollars. They towed it to a local junkyard and cut off the top of the VW…. Then they attached the VW top to the roof of the bus with plumber's tape and screws and drove off to a state park. While parked in the state park they removed the VW top, cut through the ceiling of their school bus, and then welded the VW top on.

Arizona, USA, 2001.
Photograph by Jenny Nordquist.

'Almost Willie', Quartzsite, USA,
February 2001.
Photograph by Jenny Nordquist.

In the UK, the VW camper 'scene' is mostly a show-orientated vibe.

Rikki James / UK

To say that Rikki James is a VW bus enthusiast is a major understatement. Visiting shows and rallies with Rikki, it soon becomes apparent that he is 'the man' on the VW circuit, particularly when it comes to the split-screen variety. A hugely knowledgeable, popular and energetic figure around the shows, he writes, and with a group of other enthusiasts he runs the Split Screen Van Club that meets every weekend through the summer season, as well as BWA—Buses With Attitude. The SSVC, formed in 1983 by a small group of enthusiasts to preserve and celebrate 'Splittys', now has around 1,300 members worldwide. It is a highly sociable one, with a special section for children called the "Split Screen Seedlings". "It wouldn't be possible to do all this without a very understanding wife and children."

Needless to say meanwhile, Rikki has had a range of VW buses of his own: in 1989 he bought his first Deluxe, a 1967 right hand drive 21 window Samba which he restored to his own specificiation.

Rikkis' own van now is a 1954 right hand drive Deluxe, one of the most sought-after split screen VWs. Rikki is not a VW purist, and has modified his van—lowering the suspension and adding Porsche 914 brakes to slow down the 2.6 litre engine and a Porsche 911 5 speed gearbox. "The engine seemed to take forever to run in; however that's all history now. Just to give you an idea of its performance, you can change into fifth gear at around 100 mph!!" Featuring in the VW specialist magazines and websites, as well as at more or less every VW show and rally through the summer, Rikki and his van may be special but he still drives it every day and it's a familiar sight on the roads of West London.

I probably will restore the bus's paint some day but for the moment I am happy with the way it is.

Left: Rikki James' 1954 right hand drive Deluxe—"one of the most sought after VW buses".
Courtesy Rikki James.

Right: Rikki, (right), on the way to the 2004 Volksword show.
Courtesy of www.barndoormafia.com

All this 'function', yet it still manages to arouse our senses.

Julie Breed and family / UK

I think my appreciation of the VW camper van goes right back to those heady teenage years—I was encouraged by my parents to emerge into adulthood as an independent, free-thinking individual, influenced on the way by 60s rock vinyl and the whole flower-power, hippy eccentric thing. I have always been artistic, creative, off-beat, individual and, if I'm honest, have always probably gone out of my way to provoke a reaction or turn peoples' heads. So it was a foregone conclusion that my chosen vehicle wasn't going to be a Ford Focus!

Julie's VW is a 1972 Deluxe Microbus, in chianti red and white. She found it amongst the ads in *Volksworld* after searching in vain for a more conventional vehicle large enough to carry her four children and their friends, and interesting enough to satisfy her own needs as the driver. Julie is an art teacher with a degree in graphic design; the bus works for her on many levels, from practical necessity to aesthetic appeal.

Driving a VW isn't about keeping up with the Joneses, about getting from A to B in a hurry or in comfort or luxury. It's about driving something you love with a passion and experiencing the journey. Who cares about miles to the gallon or speed or aerodynamics?

The bus had been fully restored to show-winning standard, featuring in *Volksworld* in February 2002. Whilst this makes it a truly special VW, for Julie and her family, it is an everyday vehicle. As the driver, Julie is constantly reminded of its practical shortcomings as well as its special qualities:

In spite of fighting for a gear, constantly clearing a space to see out of the windscreen and wrestling to control two tonnes of rusting metal at speed, a VW driver will always flash their headlights furiously and wave like you're one of the family when a fellow Vdubber is spotted on the road.

It's like a TARDIS—four kids, a tent the size of a marquee, clothes, pram and two dogs, yet it will still park in a standard car park space at Tescos.

Top: Julie Breed's 1972 Deluxe Microbus.

Opposite: From eldest to youngest—Sam, Madeline, Hetty and Harvey.

The van was an economical way of making the journey to wherever we wanted, whenever we wanted.

Anthony Hudson, Jenny Dale, Louise Sakula, Robert Sakula and Paul Griffith / UK

In 1980, a group of young architects and friends borrowed a VW bus and travelled by ferry from Plymouth to Santander for a three week 'architectural pilgrimage' visiting remote Romanesque churches along the northern coast of Spain. Packing the van with tents and camping equipment, the group camped on beaches and fields over-looking the sea rather than on formal sites...

Everything has to have a place, otherwise all hell breaks loose.

Louis Hudson / UK

19 year old Louis is a surfer who lives in Norfolk and surfs wherever he can. His van is a 1976 Ford Transit Mark 1 converted by Buccaneer. Of course he had always known that surfers drive VW buses, and was going to try to find one for himself, but gradually became more interested in finding something slightly less clichéd. He wanted to travel, not just surf, and needed a van that was reasonably cheap to buy. He also wanted something sufficiently 'cool', that could hold its own on any campsite or beach.

Louis searched through the small ads in his local newspaper and found the Transit—for under £1,000. The previous owner had looked after the mechanics well and gave Louis a checklist to help him look after the van, as well as a 'little red book' that itemised mileage and fuel consumption. As a result, Louis feels almost an obligation to look after the van to a similarly high standard.

Louis set about refurbishing the interior. A self-confessed perfectionist, he found the interior badly designed and made some modifications in order to make best use of the limited space. Though the image of grungy surfer holds fast, increasingly the reality is that many surfers do not live their lives in a permanent state of damp, sand-encrusted disorder, or wear that lifestyle as a badge of credibility. Having refurbished his van to a high quality, Louis prefers to leave the sand outside at the end of the day's surfing and his priorities were "a bed, a fridge and lots of cupboards".

During the summer of 2004, using *The Stormrider Guide to Europe*, Louis and his girlfriend Stacey travelled about 4,000 miles in five weeks across France, into Spain and Portugal, and home again. At around 20 to 25 mpg, the negative aspects of the van mainly revolved around fuel consumption. On a tight budget, this meant sticking carefully to the optimum speed of 50 mph. "Five miles an hour faster made a lot of difference to the cost of fuel after a while."

On his travels, motorhome owners, van owners, people camping in tents, hippies—fellow travellers young and old—appreciated the van. "It was cool in Europe because of its rarity there. And the roof helped! It is a wicked system and doubles the size of the van."

It's just like a small flat on wheels, isn't it?

Louis Hudson's 1976 Ford Transit Mark 1 Buccaneer conversion.

The first time you get in a VW bus, you feel as if you are on top of the world.

Sam and Sam Clark / UK

Sam and Sam Clark opened their restaurant Moro in 1997, now well-known for its marvellous combination of cooking from Spain and less familiar areas of the Mediterranean. The year before it opened, they toured around Spain and Morocco in a camper van.

> We already knew more or less what we were going to do with Moro—that guided the journey. The trip was to collect recipes and ideas and just soak in as much as we could from Spain and Morocco. Moro wouldn't have been Moro without the trip. We knew that when we came back we had a lot of stuff that we could put on the menu straight away. Exciting stuff, new stuff that hadn't really been seen in London before.

The couple went to Market Road in North London where, once a month, travellers would converge to buy and sell VW buses. "We weren't properly clued up—I'm not a car person. So we went to the people we liked the look of. But you can't judge a camper van by whether or not it's got nice curtains."

Though they did not find a van that they wanted, they did see a sticker displayed in a VW bus window advertising Jack's Garage where they bought their van for £1,000:

> It was called Max; the name was handed down. When you're told your car has a name, you use it. "Max needs some petrol, or Max needs some oil. Max is getting a bit hot. Max is getting a bit cold." Then when you sell it, you tell the new owner that it's called Max. It's probably still called Max today.

The couple wanted a VW for a range of reasons: being high up was the perfect travelling position and, crucially, they were self-sufficient with their own kitchen.

"We were pretty well read and had started testing out recipes; we knew where we wanted to go and what we wanted to learn. But we didn't want to go to endless cheap hotels. We wanted to have the van so we could do quite a 'budget' trip."

Having our little cooker, we could go to the markets, we could experiment along the way and cook things that were tasty. It was perfect.

The trip took them through Paris, south over the Pyrenees and on to Barcelona, around southern Spain and into Morocco, with a variety of incidents on the way, including losing their windscreen as they were heading for the Sahara.

> There are these endless single-track roads and drivers playing 'chicken' to see who would get knocked off. We were going along and, as a lorry passed us, a stone flew up and cracked our windscreen into a thousand million pieces. So we smashed it all out and thought, "If we pass somewhere to get it fixed, we'll get it done." We passed a couple of places but they wanted £200 to replace it and we thought we were being ripped off. So we didn't get one and carried on driving for the whole journey back, for three weeks without a windscreen!

I've been into Volkswagens for as long as I can remember.

Mark Hopley / UK

Mark imported his 'dream bus', a 1961 23 window Samba Deluxe, to the UK from California in August 2002. Missing the lower six inches all the way round, and most of the floor, the bus needed a fair amount of work to bring it up to the standard it is today. Now complete, it has won 15 trophies at numerous UK shows, including Best of Show at Big Bang, Best Split at Bristol, Best Modified Type 2 and Best Air-Cooled at Stonor Park, and Best of Show at the 2005 Volksworld show. The bus also featured in *Volksworld*'s summer 2005 issue.

I've been into Volkswagens for as long as I can remember. Initially my passion was for Beetles then, like most people, I moved onto buses. I now pretty much exclusively restore pre-1967 split-screen models and, above all, I am an enthusiast. I take a great deal of pride in doing as much myself as possible, as it's the only way I can be sure it's right.

Mark Hopley's completed restoration of his 1961 23 window Samba Deluxe.

It's not just a trip.
It's a journey.

Grant Dodd / UK

Grant Dodd set up Jack's Garage in London's Ladbroke Grove in 1995. Many VW owners in London and South East England either buy their vans from Grant in the first place, or take them to him to be looked after.

He first came to London from New Zealand 18 years ago and saw a job advertised in *TNT* (a magazine for New Zealanders and Australians in London) fixing camper vans in a VW garage for an Australian boss; though he had seen VW vans in New Zealand, he had never driven one. Managing workshops for other people gave him the experience and confidence to set up Jack's Garage and he has worked with VWs ever since.

Grant has had several VW vans. His first was a 1976 left hand drive Camper, bought in 1989, which he used to travel round Europe for three months. Returning to London, he sold it and bought another and travelled round Europe for a second time where, in 1990, he met his wife, Michelle.

At this point in his VW career, a van was still just a means of transport. "I was probably too young; I was just thinking of travelling." His second VW was a 1973 Type 2 1.6 Devon which he kept for two years, the third a 1974 right hand drive 1700cc Westfalia.

"When I got the '74 1700, then I was aiming for my perfect vehicle. I thought that could have been the right van but it wasn't perfect."

> Now I have the perfect van. It's a Type 2 1979 right hand drive 2 litre Westfalia. I can count on the fingers of one hand how many there are in England. One owner before me, an Australian guy who bought it new. He'd had it since 1979. I bought it from him this Christmas [2005]. I'd been looking that long. I couldn't find one anywhere. It's special.

Top: Grant at Jack's Garage with his collection of VW model toys.

Bottom: Bird's eye view of Jack's Garage.

Grant's top three:

1. a '79, because it's the last one they made and it's got all the modern technology and adjustments for that period. So I would always want a '79.

2. I want the biggest engine. I want more power. Most people go out and buy the basic 1.6. Don't you want to put your foot down and have horsepower and pass the truck in front of you? Do you want to sit in the slow lane all the time?

3. I always want right hand drive. Left hand drive is only good for Europe, though some people are just not bothered at all.

Grant says that, for most of the owners who take their vans to 'Jack's', "it's their passion, their love. It's their one vice in life probably! They tell me their stories all the time. And I fix them 100 per cent so they don't break down, so no phone calls when they are travelling."

They often ask advice when they are buying a new van. They ask me what they need to carry in spares on their travels. They ask me what kinds of things they need to know about travelling through Europe. And there's one big one: read the petrol pumps clearly. I get many phone calls every year from owners telling me they've just filled up their van with diesel and asking me 'What do I do?' (You've got to drain the whole tank out and fill it back up again. I've done it myself.)

Grant is not interested in 'show and shine' and would rather use his van as an everyday vehicle. With three small children, aged three, five and seven, Grant and Michelle plan to take more trips now: "I've only now finally bought my ideal van so the memorable trips are probably going to be with the kids from now on."

For Grant, the VW bus is the business. He uses three words when talking about them: simplicity, character, quality. "It's the quality. Durable, strong, German technology. The way they drive is superb. You are sitting on top of the front wheel so steering is just so easy, sitting high up looking down on all the traffic." The only disadvantage he knows is fuel consumption, which can be as low as 23 to 25 mpg.

Driving a camper puts a smile on your face! You just look at them and you smile. You see people smiling when they are driving them. And they all wave to each other. When you are sitting there you can actually look around; you're not in the fast lane just looking straight ahead. You are in the slow lane and enjoying the trip. It's probably why people don't mind the 1.6.

Top: Grant Dodd outside Jack's Garage.

Opposite: View of Jack's Garage.

Home away from Home The World of Camper Vans and Motorhomes

Despite all that, it was the most amazing trip.

Debbie Whitfield and Will Tomlinson / UK

Best friends Debbie and Will bought 'Willerby' from a surfer in Devon who converted the VW into a camper himself but, facing the prospect of children and "not being a surfer dude anymore", had to sell.

In the late 1990s, Will, a graphic designer who recently-graduated from Brighton University, had a brain haemorrhage; after major surgery, he recovered but had lost the power of speech, which he then had to re-learn. The pair decided to buy the van together so that they could travel to Europe in the summer of 2001. By this time, Will's speech was almost back to normal but he was not allowed to drive, so Debbie drove for the entire trip,

> except for four days on a Croatian island, where we didn't think the police would reach us. Will couldn't remember the names of places or directions very well which led to slightly stressful confusions between roundabouts and traffic lights!

They took the ferry to Calais from Dover, "pretending we were doing a day return to make it cheaper", then went to Belgium, Germany, Czech Republic, Poland, Slovakia, Hungary, Croatia, Italy and France. On their return, they sold the van to Will's parents, to "keep it in the family".

Debbie Whitfield and Will Tomlinson and their VW on tour in Europe in the summer of 2001.

Wow, the van blew up!

The Redding Family / UK

This 1990 VW Transporter belongs to Rebecca, Toby and Isabel Redding, and their parents, Elizabeth and Mark. It sleeps five "with ease", two in a pull-out bed and three, or more, in the 'Viking' pop-up roof. The van's previous owner was a surfer and most of the problems the Reddings have had with it are the result of years of sand and sea-water. The water system has a habit of harbouring air locks in the bends and kinks of the pipes, causing a recent incident. Twelve year old Rebecca tells the story:

When we got 'Gibb', she was gun-metal grey and covered with skulls, a bucketful of sand, weird 'surf-dude' stickers and, inside, an oven with a skull cover. A year's work later, she is a modern van with a fridge/freezer and a working sink.

Recently, we were on the way back home to Gloucestershire from Snowdonia, when the van started to wail like a banshee. We scrambled out and waited, shivering, for Dad to sort out the problem. "The van's not going to blow up", he said, reassuringly. Bending over the engine, he started to unscrew the water cap; it shot up in the air, followed by a jet of hot water. "Wow", said Toby, "The van blew up!"

Toby, Isabel and Rebecca Redding
in the family VW.

Although it's obviously a truck, it doesn't come across as a macho thing.

Bamber Johnson with Sue, Ruby and Archie / UK

Bamber Johnson is a builder based in North London. He drives a 1973 right hand drive VW Crew-cab. Apart from his love of VWs, for Bamber, the choice of Crew-cab was a key business decision, and he spent 18 months finding the right one.

My partner and I decided that it made it look like we weren't just ordinary builders driving a white Transit. I think it says that we've got some kind of design awareness. We do mostly interior stuff—bathrooms and kitchens. It certainly attracts attention. People see that I am using it for work and they just start talking to me about it. Everybody's brother has had one.

Volkswagen first built the Crew-cab version of the pick-up in 1958. "Other builders think I am mad for using such a nice vehicle for work but I'm pleased to be using it for what it was designed for. I don't feel precious about it because I bought it for that specific purpose."

Before the Crew-cab, the family had a 1979 Camper which Bamber, his wife, Sue, and their two children, Ruby and Archie used to go surfing. In the early days, the family would travel to Cornwall in a Ford Cortina Mark I Estate but bought a VW van "because it was more practical". The whole family slept in the van, the kids in the two suspended bunks.

"You go to Devon or Cornwall and all the surfers drive VWs. It's just the normal thing to do. You go to the campsite in your estate car and get out a tiny little two man tent, roughing it, and then all of a sudden there they are in all their luxury."

We did have some great holidays. We used to go to France every year for three sometimes four weeks in the summer. I used to save up all my holidays and then we would go off. Sue's sister used to come along as well—she had the same van. So she and her family used to come and there used to be four or five families all together at one point, all with VWs.

Now I prefer to stay somewhere with a roof and a bathroom!

Sue Johnson.

We used to go to Devon for weekends. We'd leave about 5 o'clock in the morning. We used to make up the beds and I'd carry the kids down and they'd sleep on the way. Then we'd be half way down the motorway and they'd be saying 'Are we there yet, Dad?

Volkswagen marketing brochure, 1959.
Collection of Everett Barnes.

*Right: Ruby and Archie in the family's
1979 VW Camper.*

*Bottom: Bamber Johnson in his 1973
right hand drive VW Crew-cab.*

Home away from Home The World of Camper Vans and Motorhomes

Worlds collide or worlds apart?

It's just a means of transport for those people; for us it's a way of life.

Grant Dodd, Jack's Garage.

VW marketing brochure.
Collection of Malcolm Bobbitt.

Are camper vans and motorhomes today different ends of the same spectrum or do they in fact inhabit completely different worlds? Grant Dodd, owner and proprietor of VW specialist Jack's Garage in London's Ladbroke Grove, believes that the two worlds are mutually exclusive. More than that, he says that his customers tell him time after time how motorhome owners look down on their VW buses on camp grounds the world over.

How do you bring the two together, besides the fact that you are sleeping in a vehicle? There's no comparison. We can do it all exactly the same as them for a fraction of the budget. It's like staying in a pension rather than a hotel.

For Rick Whittaker of The Motor Caravanners' Club, the VW world and the motorhome world are not so different and any difference is mostly driven by what people use their vehicles for. "Historically, the VW was the generic 'camper' and many started with it because there was little else on the market; but, they're all motorcaravans."

I do go to a lot of shows, but I go there for other reasons. I go there to buy second hand parts. And I go to them because I like the different vehicles. The people are good.

Grant Dodd, Jack's Garage.

The mobile life, full- or part-time, is not for everyone; the natural instinct apparent in many owners to flock together—a kind of non-communal community—is replaced in others by an active search for seclusion. For some owners, the prospect of joining a club goes against the very motivation for travelling in a motorhome or camper van. For others though, clubs perform a valuable role. As with many specialist automotive fraternities, many of the owners clubs for the older camper van and motorhome were formed out of the need to exchange practical information, tips on maintenance, even parts. And depending on the exact constituency of the club, owners not only correspond with each other, and meet at the rallies that are a common feature across automotive owners clubs of all types, but travel together.

The majority of makes have owners' clubs, so the range is vast, covering new and classic motorhomes, campers in the UK and RVs in the USA. The USA has 'The Good Sam Club' and 'Escapees', whose members are called SKiPs for short, each with thousands of members, and many more clubs too. The Good Sam Club holds the notion of mutual aid amongst its members as central to its existence. One of the reasons for its inception in the mid 1960s was the increasing reluctance to offer, or accept, help from strangers on the road. Just as the Tin Can Tourists earlier in the century had hung an empty soup can from their radiator caps as a badge to signify membership to one another, so members of The Good Sam Club recognise one another by the Club badge and are secure in the knowledge that they can offer, and accept, help to a fellow member in trouble at the roadside. Escapees Inc was started in 1978 by Joe and Kay Peterson. Initially an informal network of full-time RVers, by 1995, the club had become a corporation, with full-time employees, a magazine and a number of RV parks under its supervision.[21]

The Family Motor Coach Association (FMCA) is an international organisation based in Cincinnati for families with motorhomes. Founded in 1963, it has many roles including organising social activities and enabling the exchange of information. 18 families were involved at the Association's inception in 1963; now in excess of 127,000 families are members. It publishes a regular magazine, *Family Motor Coaching*. The RVIA meanwhile is the USA's national trade association representing more then 500 manufacturers and suppliers involved in the RV industry.

Meanwhile, the UK also has a large number of owner's clubs that look after the interests of owners of just about every make and model of camper van and motorhome, the old and the new. These clubs organise rallies and shows throughout the summer catering for owners and interested non-owners alike.

In its nineteenth year, 2005's Run to the Sun brought 3,500 vehicles and crowds of around 100,000 people to Cornwall, making it the largest custom car, Volkswagen and dance festival in Europe.[22] The surfing correspondent for local paper, *The Western Morning News*, reported that "the queue of cars attempting to get into Newquay stretched... for miles. Many of the classic car owners who had turned up for the rally were from the South West, but there were plenty there who had come from as far afield as Nottingham and South Wales." As with most custom vehicle rallies, one of the central elements is a 'Show 'n' Shine', during which enthusiasts exhibit their prize possessions. Whilst the Show 'n' Shine is not for some owners who prefer to drive their buses on a regular basis, many find these events allow them to see a whole range of rare and unusual vans, some of which have had many hours and often a great deal of money spent on restoring them to their original condition.

Sarah Tyrrell and Kim Hedges are sisters. Sarah drives a VW bus while Kim owns a Swift Gazelle with her husband David.

I love the van; I would still love the van even if I couldn't sleep in it. Children point at it at zebra crossings and couriers say "Hey, nice van, man."

Sarah Tyrrell / UK

Kim's van is a vehicle for camping and she needs it to be a 'home from home'. We sleep in our van, but when we're camping, we spend our time outside. If we go somewhere we don't know, we'll use a campsite. But we like more rural places, more spit and sawdust.

Sarah had driven a VW Beetle in Los Angeles for four years and, when it was time to return to the UK, she was talked into selling the Beetle, which she loved, and buying a VW bus to ship all her and her boyfriend's belongings back to the UK.

She bought the van from a surfer who had lived in it for two years. He wanted $2,000 for it; Sarah's budget did not stretch that far. But because he felt that the van was 'going home', the surfer sold it to her for $1,300; he rang more or less every day before she left to make sure that plans for its safe return were going well.

The van cost $1,000 to ship, filled with bikes, photo albums and belongings; the logic was that it would probably cost about the same for that amount of space to ship their belongings anyway.

The van was late arriving so Sarah called the shipper and found out that while the boat was going through the Panama Canal, some of its cargo had to be removed to get it through; the container with her van in it happened to be off-loaded and sat on the side of the Panama Canal for two months. Eventually the van arrived and Sarah went to pick it up from Tilbury Docks.

At this point, Sarah still could not see what others saw in the van. The front had been stripped but not restored—"body-wise it didn't look pretty". And, as it had not been driven for a while, it was run down mechanically. She got it back to Bournemouth and took it to a local VW garage. The mechanic looked at it, recognised it as something special and offered to buy it. She took it to another; he offered to buy it. As time wore on, and encouraged by the response she was getting, Sarah began to realise what a great van she had and decided to have it restored. It is now back to its original colour and the interior is as it was, with its original panelling and seats.

Sarah Tyrrell's VW bus, now restored.

Home away from Home The World of Camper Vans and Motorhomes

If you thought that buying a house was difficult, you should try choosing a motorhome as a first time buyer!

Kim and David Hedges / UK

In the airline industry, Kim and David Hedges had spent most of their careers seeing far-flung parts of the world. So, as retirement approached, they decided that is was time to start enjoying the UK.

As a teenager, David had stayed in a motorhome with friends on many canoeing trips and soon discovered the freedom that they offered while Kim always enjoyed the outdoor life and spent many happy days as a child in her aunt's caravan. After hiring a motorhome for a touring holiday in Scotland, they decided to buy their own and began the task of narrowing down the field from an overwhelming choice.

Kim and David Hedges' 1999 Swift Gazelle F59 on holiday.

Kim and David bought their 1999 Swift Gazelle F59 motorhome, now named 'Glenda', in August 2004. Trying to get away at least once a month, they have now explored a great deal of the UK and have just returned from a trip around France. The couple are planning a trip touring the Rockies in September 2006. They have modified the vehicle since they bought it, installing an improved suspension system and adding a specially manufactured rack to carry a motorbike, which they use to explore wherever they happen to end up, using the Swift as a 'base'.

David does any minor repairs and modifications himself; any major work and routine servicing is left to the professionals.

It's nice to 'personalise' your motorhome...

Kim and David Hedges' 1999 Swift Gazelle F59.

Strange bedfellows

Images from the collections of Malcolm Bobbitt, Kate Trant, Martin Watts/Classic Camper Club.

Home cooking

Bran Muffins Jarlsberg

When we want to hit the road very early, I assemble the ingredients the night before, bake these while we're getting ready to roll, then serve them on the go with hot coffee. They are rich and moist enough to be eaten plain, without butter, and hearty enough to constitute a real stick-to-the-ribs breakfast.

½ c. flour
¼ c. miller's bran
⅓ c. brown sugar
¼ c. chopped nuts
¼ c. butter, softened
16-oz. package date-bread mix
1 c. milk
small apple, chopped
¼ c. oil
1 egg
¾ c. shredded Jarlsberg cheese

In a small bowl mix the butter, flour and sugar until crumbly. Set aside. In a large bowl combine remaining ingredients. Mix with a wooden spoon just until well blended with no dry particles. Spoon the mixture into paper-lined muffin cups, filling no more than 2/3 full, and sprinkle with the crumb mixture. Bake at 400° about 20 minutes or until they test done. Cool in the pan five minutes, then remove to a cooking rack. Serve warm-m-m-m. This makes a dozen regular-size muffins.

Brunswick Stew

Let this simmer on the galley stove all afternoon on a chilly day or use a pressure cooker to speed cooking. The meat must fall apart into shreds. This makes a huge batch that will serve 12 to 20, so it's great for campground potluck suppers.

2 lbs. chicken thighs, skinned
2 lbs. lean chuck
2 lbs. lean pork
8 c. water
3 lg. onions, diced
46-oz. can tomato juice
4 cans, 1lb. each, cream-style corn
16-oz. can green limes
3 t. vinegar
1 t. dried sage
Salt, pepper
Hot sauce to taste

Choose very lean beef and pork roasts and have the butcher grind them coarsely. Bring the meats, water and onion to a boil in a large, heavy kettle over a high flame. Reduce the heat, cover and simmer until meats are very tender. Remove the thighs with tongs, discard the bones, and chop the meat. Return chicken to the stew with the remaining ingredients, and cook over medium heat, stirring often to prevent scorching, until it's well heated. Serve in soup bowls with a hearty whole-wheat bread, apple butter, raw vegetable sticks, and gingerbread with vanilla sauce for dessert.

These recipes are from Cooking Aboard
Your RV by Janet Groene, Ragged
Mountain Press, 1993.
Reproduced with the permission of
The McGraw-Hill Companies.

Endnotes

1. Barker, F Aldred, *First Experiences with Motor Car and Camera*, Matthews and Brooke, 1911.

2. Barker, F Aldred, *Camping with Motor-Car and Camera*, J M Dent & Sons, 1913, pp. 8-15.

3. Barker, *Camping*, p. 284.

4. Ferguson, Melville F, *Motor Camping on Western Trails*, Century Co, 1924.

5. Jessup, Elon, *The Motor Camping Book*, G P Putnam's Sons, 1921, p. 7

6. Dickinson, Joy Wallace, "King of the Road", *The Lake Sentinel*, 20 February 2000.

7. Forsyth, B, "They Leave the Driving to Themselves", *The Sacramento Union*, 6 September 1970.

8. Counts, Dorothy and David, *Over the Next Hill: An Ethnography of RVing Seniors in North America*, Broadview Press Ltd, 2001 (2nd edition), p. 102.

9. "Overnight shopping", *Motor Caravan*, April 2005

11. "The story so far", *Motor Caravan*, December 2004.

11. Counts, *Over the Next Hill*, p. 145.

12. Counts explain how "RVers warned us that it is impossible to generalize about the "average RVer" because each of them is unique... many RVers see their resistance to classification as a virtue and treasure their differences."

13. Counts, *Over the Next Hill*, p. 18.

14. Counts, *Over the Next Hill*.

15. Maney, Kevin, "The year according to eBay", *USA TODAY*, 29 December 2004 (www.usatoday.com).

16. For example, "Even if there were an agreed-on definition of a full-time RVer, no census of them would be accurate. Many have no permanent home base. They use the address of a friend or relative to license their vehicles and get driver's licenses, register to vote, and pay their taxes. "Full-time RVer" does not appear on Canadian or US census forms. Full-timers are, in effect, an invisible population, and many of them prefer it that way. Many have no interest in being enumerated. They fear that if "the government" finds out about them it will tax them or otherwise destroy their lifestyle and their freedom." Counts, *Over the Next Hill*, p. 57.

17. Greg's fiancée to Jack, *Meet the Fockers*, 2004.

18. Wolinsky, Cary, "America's Largest Parking Lot", *National Geographic*, January 2001.

19. Counts, *Over the Next Hill*, p. 90.

20. Pallidini, J and Dubin, B, *Roll Your Own: The Complete Guide to Living in a Truck, Bus, Van or Camper*, Macmillan Publishing Co, Inc, 1974, p. 76.

21. Counts, *Over the Next Hill*, 1996, p. 44.

22. "Sun shines for gathering of custom cars", *The Western Morning News*, 30 May 2005.

Chapter Three

All Mod Cons

Malcolm Bobbitt

Mobile developments

> ... *the motor caravan is an up-and-running leisure vehicle and no longer an oddity on our roads.*
>
> "Motor Caravans—the new leisure vehicle", *Motor,* October 1973.

While the motorhome is perceived as being a largely recent development, its conception can be traced to the formative years of the twentieth century.

For the more adventurous traveller in times past, the thought of visiting resorts, either at home or abroad, and being tied to a single location was all too restrictive. Limiting, too, was being bound to a hotel or guest house, which meant having to endure unwanted regimentation. The answer, it seemed, was to go self-catering, though the cost of renting a property was often prohibitive. All the more acceptable was a caravan holiday, which in essence offered hardly little more sophistication than living under canvas.

Owning a caravan and towing it around the country made more sense, notwithstanding the fact that the constant process of hitching and unhitching was wearisome. Driving from place to place, site to site, with caravan in tow gave cause for some misgivings, not least negotiating narrow lanes and hilly routes. Not everyone mastered the art of towing, especially reversing, which had to be avoided at all costs.

More practical was the notion of combining caravan and motor vehicle. Instead of trailing a makeshift home around in cumbersome fashion, having a permanent roof above one's head seemed all the more practical. This did away with routes, terrain and overnight stops that were not conducive to car and trailer: the nomad instinct was satisfied.

While the motorhome is perceived as being a largely recent development, its conception can be traced to the formative years of the twentieth century. Imagine the furore, therefore, when, around 1910, a growling monstrosity, complete with folding beds and a host of ancillary equipment left London's Hyde Park to embark on a world tour. The fact that this colossus, built on a 25 hp Panhard-Levassor chassis, managed to reach snow-stricken St Petersburg is beyond a miracle. Even more unbelievable, having been abandoned in the Russian wasteland, it was rescued and returned to London, where it was displayed at the Royal Agricultural Hall to immense curiosity.

It was only a matter of time before other motorhome designs emerged. In France a maison automobile was exhibited in 1904 in conjunction with the Société Nationale des Beaux Arts. The Manchester based Belsize Motor Company built a six berth motorhome of extreme proportions to the order of Liverpool businessman J B Mallalieu whose intent it was to tour the British Isles. Mallalieu's motorhome with its washroom, WC and running water, even by today's standards was impressive at almost 22 feet in length, 6 ½ feet wide and more than 10 feet in height. Weighing four tons, the speed of the Belsize with its solid rubber tyres seldom exceeded walking pace.

The concept attracted the attention of a number of pioneer motorists including Arthur du Cros (whose father William Harvey had helped develop the world's tyre industry) who, in 1909, invested £2,000, a sum today equal to £200,000 in an Austin-chassied motorhome. The 40 hp vehicle was luxuriously equipped with electric lighting supplied from on-board batteries, pumped water, and an intercom system that linked the vehicle's living quarters with the driver's cab. L H Hounsfield of Trojan fame also anticipated the virtues of the motorhome with a formidable six wheeled pantechnicon, while Sir Malcolm Campbell used a converted single-decker coach in which to live while racing and attempting the world speed water record. In America the first motorhomes took the form of converted Model T Fords, a far cry from later developments.

Other offerings were bizarre to say the least, such as the streamlined Light Cruiser from Road Yachts, Clifford Dawtrey's Lounge car, and G C Gore Crellin's 'Highway Yacht' designed to accommodate eight passengers and a crew of three on a Guy six-wheel lorry chassis. Motorhomes were undeniably slow and unwieldy and, had it not been for two factors, could have easily fallen into obscurity. The first was at the behest of Bill Riley and his son who converted their 1909 Talbot to provide sleeping accommodation. Riley's theory was simple: he anticipated retiring and wanted to travel in a style that was simple yet efficient. The conversion of the touring saloon held a number of limitations, but when *The Autocar* carried a feature on it, several enquiries for similar conversions were received. Later the Rileys bought into H A Eccles' Birmingham haulage business to become Britain's principal motorhome manufacturer.

The second factor was the onset of war in 1914 which saw the development of the armoured car and field ambulance, as well as general use of motor vehicles. The Red Cross used motor caravans to great effect which helped to cultivate the modern motorhome.

While motorhomes achieved a measure of popularity during the 1920s and 30s, demand was minimal compared to trailer caravan sales. It was only in the postwar years that motorhomes achieved serious recognition, and then largely as a result of Germany's development of Volkswagen. Having visited Volkswagen's factory at Wolfsburg in British-occupied Germany during the wake of World War Two, Dutch motor vehicle importer Ben Pon was intrigued to see a number of Beetle-engined trolleys transporting components around the works. The sight of them encouraged the Dutchman to develop the idea for a multi-purpose commercial vehicle which evolved as Volkswagen's Type 2 Transporter, now a design icon familiar on roads throughout the world.

1951 German VW marketing brochure.
Collection of Everett Barnes.

The ending of hostilities brought a renewed sense of hope and freedom as well as a concerted call for prosperity, social change and the rebuilding of societies and communities. The effects of postwar austerity nevertheless slowed the process: shortages of raw materials hampered industrial reconstruction, rationing remained, and queues for food were a way of life. Holidays for all but the wealthiest of people were little more than dreams, but for the more resourceful, acquiring ex-military vehicles and converting them to camping cars provided a means of potential freedom, as long as there was petrol available to run them.

Customers seeking proprietary motorhomes had to wait until the early 1950s before their hopes were fulfilled—even then they were initially reliant on Volkswagen's air-cooled Type 2 Transporter. It had been left to Germany to devise the modern motorhome and thereby satisfy a willing and growing market. When the Transporter with its now recognisable split-screen cab, striking v-shape frontal definition and large VW roundel was adopted by the German caravan manufacturer Westfalia for conversion to its 'Camping Box' it was met with instant success. Thus the "brick on wheels", as it was sometimes unkindly known, became the impetus for other vehicle and caravan manufacturers to build on Volkswagen and Westfalia's success: a new industry was born, but it took time and social change for it to mature.

Volkswagen-based camper vans proliferated with the introduction of the second series Transporter. The vehicle's revised styling summoning it to be universally known as the Bay Window because of its wide and curved one piece windscreen. Indeed as each new model of Transporter appeared, it became the base vehicle for a multitude of conversions courtesy of motorhome manufacturers universally.

The prospect of buying a vehicle to serve as daily transport while doubling as a home from home in a trice, was a popular one. Who needed the bother and expense of a trailer caravan—which might only be used for a few weeks of the year? Conversion specialists were quick to seize upon a variety of vehicles on which to perform their art: Austins, Bedfords, Citroëns, Commers, Fiats, Fords, Land Rovers, Mercedes, Morrises, Peugeots, Renaults and Volvos were soon to be seen carrying caravan-like structures. Social change and expectation has meant that early postwar motorhomes with their undeniable austerity, lack of performance and limited living accommodation have evolved into something far more sophisticated within a relatively short period of time.

America, too, witnessed the motorhome revolution. Here Volkswagen again led the way with a variety of conversions, Sportsmobile's treatment of the Split Screen Transporter being one. The American market had an appetite for something far more accommodating, and as trailer caravans had already grown to leviathan proportions to incorporate every conceivable luxury, it was only a matter of time before similarly sized motorhomes appeared on the scene. Their arrival in 1966 was in the style of the vast Winnebago, a self-sufficient home on wheels.

Westfalia marketing brochure, 1957.
Collection of Greg Noble.

Holidays for all but the wealthiest of people were little more than dreams.

The 1970s and 80s were the boom years in European motorhome development. This was a period when new trends were being set to establish the motorhome as being a dedicated and purpose-built vehicle. From what were essentially run-of-the-mill commercial vehicles converted to offer no more than a compromise between camping and caravanning, emerged the designer motorhome. Features such as tables and seats that converted into beds affording questionable comfort, and barest provision of cooking and washing utensils, gave way to ingenious self-containment. Courtesy of inventive minds that were not afraid of exploring new technology, the motorhome adopted a new and exciting identity, which meant that the new generation of vehicles were luxuriously equipped with built-in kitchens and washrooms.

Following the American trend of building self-sufficiency into the motorhome, names such as the German Hymermobile emerged to offer previously unseen levels of quality and sophistication. This was also a period when increasing use was made of specific base vehicles, such as the Ford Transit, Leyland Sherpa, Bedford CF, Toyota Hi-Ace, Mercedes and Fiat, all of which gave motorhome designers greater flexibility in devising more customer-orientated vehicles.

Growing prosperity, increasing leisure time and a desire to extend the boundaries of travel meant that the motorhome developed as an important market in its own right. Motorhome dealers and converters proliferated, and with growing competition, the cost of buying a vehicle, new or previously used, became affordable.

1968 Winnebago.
Courtesy of Winnebago Industries, Inc.

Whilst panel van conversions, with either fixed, rising or high top roofs, remained a popular choice in the compact motorhome market, coachbuilt vehicles achieved popularity because they offered much more in the way of interior accommodation and layout with emphasis on customisation and equipment.

Increasing demand for motorhomes summoned new criteria in design and build techniques courtesy of manufacturers throughout Europe and America. Whilst panel van conversions, with either fixed, rising or high top roofs (the latter types often providing high level bunks mainly for use by children), remained a popular choice in the compact motorhome market, coachbuilt vehicles achieved popularity because they offered much more in the way of interior accommodation and layout with emphasis on customisation and equipment. Build techniques moved away from assembling traditional caravan-type structures. Instead, motorhome manufacturers constructed purpose-designed monocoque bodies from glass reinforced plastic (GRP) on specific chassis-cabs to afford a wealth of configurations aimed at satisfying customer demand. A range of body styles based on common themes could be offered to include overcab layouts, which maximise sleeping accommodation or storage space, and low profile types which achieve enhanced styling and aerodynamics.

Coachbuilt motorhomes have in some instances benefited from advancing chassis technology. Manufacturers of some of the more expensive and luxurious types of motorhome have adopted the AL-KO chassis arrangement to provide vehicles with a lower centre of gravity. Introduced in 1979, AL-KO replaced the original manufacturer's chassis with a lightweight, galvanised steel chassis conversion, using state-of-the art engineering techniques to significantly improve ride comfort, road holding and to allow increased payloads. An additional benefit is that the motorhome's plumbing and electrical wiring is installed within the chassis void, which can also be used to provide increased storage capacity. AL-KO chassis are designed to be compatible with the majority of base vehicles used by motorhome manufacturers, and replaces the proprietary chassis structure of the cab.

A more recent development is the A-class motorhome. This is in effect a large coachbuilt vehicle built on a chassis cowl—with cab and body being of the same width—combining to offer the most luxury accommodation. Of coach-like proportions, A-class motorhomes are offered in a variety of sizes and enjoy a popular following amongst motorhome owners intent on long duration touring. Such vehicles offer spaciousness with roomy living quarters, bespoke kitchens and washrooms. Like the larger coachbuilts, these vehicles often have an abundance of storage space to include garage areas designed to accommodate bicycles, motor scooters and outdoor equipment.

In the USA, the Winnebago theme has been adopted by a number of motorhome manufacturers. These vehicles are huge by European standards and, powered by turbo diesel engines as large as 8.5 litres, are offered in sizes of up to 40 feet in length. Being designed for long duration vacations, it is usual for these vehicles to incorporate slide-out compartments that substantially increase a vehicle's accommodation capacity when moored at camping parks. It is not unusual to see them trailing a modestly sized car for use while the motorhome is parked, others even have a built-in garage in which to house a car whilst travelling from site to site.

B and C class motorhomes refer mainly to American terminology, the former being equivalent to panel van conversions, the latter to coachbuilts. Fifth wheel trailers are essentially articulated motorhomes that attach to a tractor unit and which can be disconnected for long-term mooring, the truck allowing for day-to-day travel. Dismountables, also popular in America, have found favour in Europe and are hybrids insomuch that the coachbuilt living accommodation is removable from the base vehicle, itself usually a pick-up truck.

A far cry from their forebears, modern motorhomes represent state of the art technology. In addition to innovative coachbuilding methods employing contemporary styling and streamlining, modern handling characteristics and performance levels are wholly commensurate with today's road and driving conditions. Innovation does not stop here: on certain models air conditioning and central heating can be taken for granted while other features may well include a dishwasher, microwave cooker and amply-sized refrigerator and freezer. Moreover, self-contained washrooms with separate showers and flushing toilets are no longer classed as luxuries while home entertainment such as flat-screen televisions, DVD players and digital sound systems are commonplace accessories.

Whether it be in the most prestigious motorhome designed for prolonged touring, or a compact type in which to escape the trials of daily life for a weekend or so, never has it been so easy to make one's life home away from home.

Hymer Caravano, early 1960s.
Courtesy of Hymer AG.

Airstream Classic

Late 1970s / USA

The Classic Motor home introduced Airstream owners to a new realm of travel luxury. The interior boasted a comfortable convertible lounge, smart swivel chair and hide-away dining table. All appliances and electronics were state-of-the art and 'elegant'.

The 1979 sales literature read:

Their powerful 454 cubic inch engines are rarin' to go. Their lightweight, aerodynamic bodies stand ready to whisk you around curves, past gas pumps, through rough terrain. And their plush interiors are waiting to surround you in comfort and luxury. Motor Homes by Airstream: A first-rate idea from the first name in trailers!

Airstream Classic Motorhome, 1983.
Courtesy of Airstream, Inc.

Auto-Sleepers Clubman

Early 1990s / UK

Arguably the classic of compact European motorhomes, Auto-Sleepers' Clubman set a standard by which other motorhomes were judged when it was introduced in 1992. Designed around Volkswagen's T4 front-wheel drive Transporter chassis-cab, the Clubman was an immediate success, customers being able to choose either a 2.0 litre petrol engine or a 2.4 litre diesel engine.

When a 2.4 litre petrol engine was eventually offered it gave improved performance, but it was the 2.5 litre turbo diesel, with optional manual or automatic transmission that proved to be the most popular.

A little under 18 feet long, the Clubman is a well equipped two-berth motorhome having a wealth of features including a kitchen with luxuries such as a stainless steel drainer, fridge and built-in oven and hob. There is a separate washroom with toilet and shower facilities while the living area is spaciously appointed. The interior layout with its side settees easily transforms to either a double bed or two singles, and there is still plenty of storage space. Add to this running hot water, warm air heating, large sliding side windows and the single-piece monocoque GRP body which required little in terms of maintenance, the Clubman easily remained a market leader until it went out of production in 2004.

The interior layout with its side settees easily transforms to either a double bed or two singles, and there is still plenty of storage space.

*Auto-Sleepers Clubman.
Collection of Martin Watts/
Classic Camper Club.*

Bedford Dormobile

Early 1950s / UK

Of all British-built motorised caravans, amongst the most popular was the Bedford Dormobile. The vehicle's contemporary appearance was characterised by its box-like shape, sliding front doors and neat homely-looking rear circular side windows. Bedford Dormobiles date from 1952, the design allegedly stemming from the fact that one of Martin Walter's directors, Spencer Apps, anticipated the need for a bed-on-wheels after seeing people queuing at Channel ports and having to sleep, somewhat uncomfortably, in their cars whilst waiting for ferries.

From relatively austere early postwar Bedfords came more luxurious models fitted with elevating roofs and Dormatic seat conversions. Splendid comfort arrived in the shape of Bedford's Dormobile Romany which could be specified in a number of options, including a long wheelbase model. As increasing numbers of customers discovered the joys that motorhomes afforded, so Dormobile's business expanded to the point that it was necessary to move to a purpose-built factory employing large-scale production facilities. What made the Bedford Dormobile so successful was its reasonable purchase price, from around £700 to £900 (equivalent today to between £18,000 and £23,000) according to specification, and its 35 mpg fuel economy. By the late 1960s, Dormobile had emerged as Britain's most popular motorhome.

Bottom left: Bedford Dormobile marketing brochure, 1957.
Collection of Kate Trant.

Bottom right: Dormobile marketing brochure, 1966. Collection of Kate Trant.

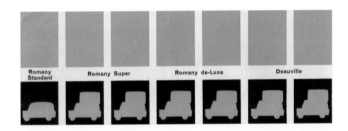

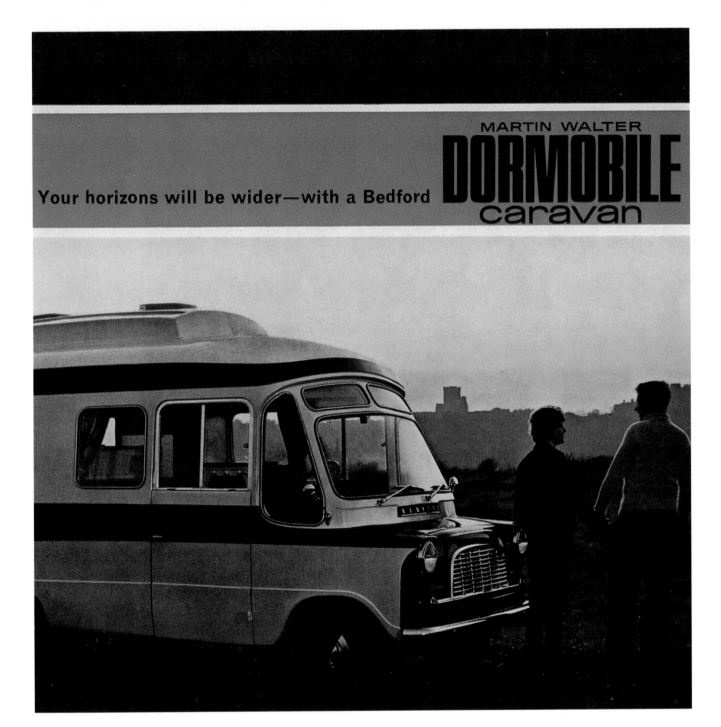

Far from the madding crowd.... Just think of the advantages of the Dormobile Caravan. No caravan parks are necessary... drive it to any accessible place you choose.... Practical in design and extremely economical, this new model offers car performance plus caravan accommodation.

Travel where you will... you're at home with a Dormobile Romany.

Top: Bedford Dormobile Romany
marketing brochure.
Collection of Kate Trant.

Bottom: Bedford Dormobile Romany marketing
brochure, 1964.
Collection of Kate Trant.

Bessacarr E700 Range

Contemporary / UK

Offering the ultimate in home from home touring, Bessacarr is at the forefront of the luxury motorhome market. When it comes to the E700 range, which is built on Fiat's long wheelbase 2.8 litre turbo diesel Ducato chassis, it is all a matter of style. Starting at a fraction over 21 feet in length, these motorhomes are hardly compact, and therefore afford much in the way of spaciousness.

The low profile coachwork is built from GRP and benefits from plentiful storage lockers. Access to the interior is eased by virtue of a fold-out step and, once inside the living quarters, there is to be found a wealth of luxury equipment to include a fully fitted kitchen with fridge/freezer and an abundance of storage space. The bathroom is also comprehensively equipped and has a circular shower cubicle.

Motorhomes the like of Bessacarr have materialised out of strong competition from other European manufacturers, both in terms of overall design, use of modern weight-saving materials, and innovative ideas when it comes to layout.

Bottom left: Bessacarr E760 rear view. Courtesy of The Swift Group.

Bottom right: Bessacarr E795. Courtesy of The Swift Group.

Top and left: Bessacarr E760 interior.
Courtesy of The Swift Group.

Bottom: Bessacarr E765 interior.
Courtesy of The Swift Group.

Bluebird Highwayman

Late 1950s / UK

During the late 1950s caravan manufacturer Bluebird realised the importance of the motorhome market and introduced their Highwayman model, designed by Bill Knott. This was a compact motor caravan, box-like in shape and, because of its dimensions, was considered easy to manoeuvre. This really was the motorhome for the popular market and, owing to its construction, which included a raised body that extended over the cab to give added storage space or another berth, afforded plentiful and spacious accommodation for the smaller family. The Highwayman was also inexpensive at £870 (£23,000 today) which added to its appeal and helped determine buoyant sales.

The demand for the Bluebird was largely in response to powerful marketing conducted by Peter Duff, the energetic owner of Crofton Garages which was the motorhome's main agent. Sales of the Bluebird Highwayman reached worldwide status when vehicles were exported to the United States, some 2,800 being sold there between 1961 and the end of the decade, by which time the American appetite was mainly for larger and more powerful vehicles.

Bluebird was eventually merged with Sprite Caravans, after which the firm was renamed Caravans International or Ci, with Peter Duff as the managing director of the new company.

"This really was the motorhome for the popular market."

Sales of the Bluebird Highwayman reached worldwide status when vehicles were exported to the United States, some 2,800 being sold there between 1961 and the end of the decade....

Bluebird Highwayman on a Commer chassis.
Collection of Martin Watts/
Classic Camper Club.

Calthorpe Home Cruiser

Late 1950s / UK

Calthorpe Home Cruiser
marketing brochure, 1962.
Collection of Martin Watts/
Classic Camper Club.

Maurice Calthorpe unveiled his Bedford-based 10 to 12 cwt Home Cruiser to an enthusiastic market at London's 1957 Ideal Homes Exhibition. In addition to Bedford, other vehicles could be made available for the Calthorpe conversion, including the Ford Thames and Austin's popular Omnivan. A particular feature of Calthorpe's conversion was its very peculiar yet robust looking domed metal elevating roof which added both height and natural light to the vehicle's interior. The Calthorpe roof, incidentally, was advertised as being completely weatherproof and could be raised within several seconds. It was also adopted by a number of motorhome converters, including Slumberwagen, either as standard or optional equipment.

The Calthorpe Home Cruiser was noted for its high standard of finish and quality furnishings. Specifications boasted fine wood interior fittings that included a full-length wardrobe, a cooker with twin burners and a grill, and 12 volt lighting. The quality was no doubt owing to the fact that the conversions were actually carried out by the highly respected caravan manufacturer F Stuart & Sons of Shepperton in Middlesex until the late 1960s.

> For weekends or longer periods away from home, the Calthorpe Home Cruiser offers wonderful accommodation for four. Completely self-contained, attractively-designed the Home Cruiser has an all metal elevating roof that gives comfortable headroom and increased interior space.

Left: Calthorpe Home Cruiser stand at
1961 Motor Show.
Collection of Martin Watts/
Classic Camper Club.

Bottom: Ford 'Holiday Adventurers' marketing
brochure, 1961, showing the Calthorpe Home
Cruiser based on the Ford Thames.
Collection of Kate Trant.

Caraversions HiTop

Early 1960s / UK

Caraversions of Lexham Gardens Mews, London W8, produced a most odd elevated roof design that could be fitted to a number of vehicles, though it was primarily intended for the Volkswagen. Designed as a hard-top loft arrangement, the conversion raised the height of the Volkswagen to 8 foot 2 inches, which meant that the vehicle's handling characteristics would have been substantially different to the more usual VW Transporter or motorhome. Nevertheless, Caraversions assured potential customers that the stability of vehicles so fitted would not be compromised, that the motorhome's top speed would be no less than 59 mph, and that fuel consumption would not drop below 30 mpg.

Built into the HiTop were two folding single berths, one at either end of the structure. When not used for sleeping accommodation the folded bunks doubled as additional kitchen or stowage space. Within the body of the motorhome, the rear compartments seats converted to a double bed while those at the front afforded additional seating accommodation.

Luxurious fittings included individual lighting to each bed and seat while the kitchen featured a stainless steel sink, Electrolux refrigerator, a cooker with two burners and grill, and a container for 12 gallons of fresh water.

Add to this stowage for crockery, cutlery and two gas bottles, not to mention louvre windows in the HiTop canopy to provide daylight and ventilation, the package adds up as being very acceptable, even if somewhat cumbersome. For all this though, sales proved to be negligible.

The HiTop has been designed and built UP to a standard and not DOWN to a price.

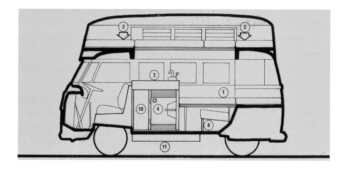

HiTop marketing brochure, early 1960s.
Collection of Malcolm Bobbitt.

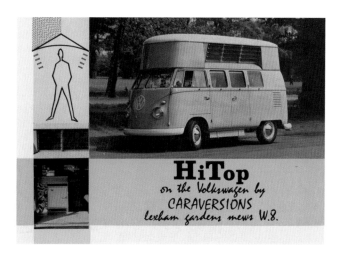

Ci Autohomes Highwayman

1970s / UK

After the Bluebird, the Highwayman theme was continued when Ci Caravans, later to become Ci Motorised, changed its name to Ci Autohomes in the 1970s. At the time, the firm's motorhomes were enjoying enviable sales, and none more so than those built on the Commer chassis which, compared to Ford's Transit, was showing its age.

The latest build techniques used within the caravan industry meant that motorhome production benefited from what was known as bonded construction, Ci being the first manufacturer to adopt the procedure. It was a wise move because today, it remains *the* technique used in the motorhome industry.

When Leyland introduced its Sherpa to rival the Ford Transit, Ci was the first motorhome producer to specify the vehicle. Trials with the Sherpa won praise from the media, such was the motorhome's design, build and interior appointment, which provided unsurpassed spaciousness and comfort. There was, however, some concern about the vehicle's handling characteristics which produced a measure of roll on winding roads and when cornering. Subsequent designs based on the Sherpa proved good for sales, and customers quickly acclimatised to the vehicle's idiosyncratic road manners.

Ci Highwayman marketing brochure.
Collection of Martin Watts/
Classic Camper Club.

Citroën H Type

Late 1940s / France

Conspicuous by its bizarre appearance, Citroën's front-wheel drive H type van was introduced in 1947. Beloved by French, Belgian and Dutch traders, it was the popular choice for motorhome conversion by thousands of Europeans. The vehicle, with its utilitarian stance, combined protruding headlights and corrugated panels to resemble a construction worker's hut on wheels. It shares its four-cylinder, 1911 cc drive train with the renowned Traction Avant that made its debut in 1934, and later the iconic DS of 1955. A range of design configurations include short and long wheelbase variants in addition to those having high top roofs. There were pick-up trucks with de-mountable bodies, breakdown wagons, ambulances, buses, mobile shops and kitchens, and motorhomes courtesy of specialist coachbuilders like Neba of The Netherlands. Because of its shape and style, the H van lends itself to easy conversion, enabling enthusiastic owners to go to extreme lengths to achieve levels of sophistication on a par with those of leading converters.

Remaining in production until 1981, examples of H vans are to be found in abundance so that motorhome conversions have become a familiar sight throughout Europe. Some owners have gone as far as adding a trailer to their motorhome, in the form of a suitably customised cab-less H van to afford the ultimate in camping units.

Top: Citroën H Type.
Collection of Malcolm Bobbitt.

Bottom and opposite: Citroën H Type.
Collection of Martin Watts/
Classic Camper Club.

WEU 145L

Coachmen Leprechaun

Contemporary / USA

At 29 feet in length, the coachbuilt Leprechaun is modest by American standards. It is what the Americans refer to as a C-class motorhome insomuch that it is a coachbuilt model with overcab.

Dating from 1997, the Leprechaun is built on the Ford E350 chassis and is powered by a 7.3 litre turbo diesel engine mated to a four-speed automatic gearbox. As might be expected of an engine of this size, it is thirsty, even when being modestly driven.

The interior of the motorhome allows for six berths including a fixed rear bed and another in the overcab compartment. There are separate dining and lounge areas, and the kitchen is built at an angle to make best use of the available space. Galley equipment includes a refrigerator and microwave cooker in addition to a conventional oven and hob. The bathroom, too, is fully equipped with shower room and toilet. Add to this a side awning and plenty of storage space, and the Leprechaun easily provides for long distance and long duration travel.

Courtesy of Coachmen RV.

Country Coach Inspire 360

Contemporary / USA

Introduced for 2006, the American Country Coach Inspire 360 is available in sizes from 36 feet to 40 feet in length to provide the ultimate in motorhome travel.

Large even by American standards, the Country Coach is powered by an 8.8 litre turbo diesel 400 hp Caterpillar engine with fully automatic transmission. Technical details include fully independent all-round air suspension and air brakes. For the family on the move, this really is a mobile home: luxury features include air conditioning, fully fitted galley, bathroom and living quarters. In addition to self-contained plumbing arrangements that include 88 gallon fresh water and 50 gallon waste water tanks, there are facilities such as built-in dishwasher and clothes washer-dryer.

Entertainment is provided by high quality radio and audio equipment as well as a choice of 27 inch or 32 inch flat screen television.

In American style, the Country Coach has a powered slide-out arrangement to provide additional living and sleeping quarters.

For the family on the move, this really is a mobile home...

Top: Country Coach range
marketing brochure.

Bottom: Country Coach Inspire 360 marketing
brochure.

Danbury

Early 1960s / Contemporary
Brazil, France & UK

THE 'DANBURY' WITH OPTIONAL ELEVATING ROOF
(ARTISTS IMPRESSION)

*Top: Danbury marketing brochure, 1969.
Collection of Malcolm Bobbitt.*

*Bottom: Danbury Rio, 2005.
Courtesy of Danbury Motorcaravans.*

The Danbury name is inextricably linked with the classic Volkswagen, having undertaken conversions since the early 1960s.

The firm now offers a number of smaller campers on a variety of chassis, including Renault and Fiat.

Danbury sells two classic VW Type 2 Transporter campers (Diamond and Rio) that are built in Brazil, the model having been withdrawn from German production in 1979. The Diamond and Rio are identically priced, both are specified with left or right hand steering, the latter commanding a £1,000 premium. The models differ mainly in their interior layout and, for those customers requiring the ultimate appointment, optional equipment includes: an elevated roof, external luggage and bike racks, awning, nose-mounted spare wheel, lowered suspension (only when alloy wheels are specified), paint colours to customer choice, portable toilet, cabinet-enclosed television and DVD player.

Additionally, Danbury provides conversions on Fiat and Renault vehicles, both being new for 2005. The Fiat models comprise the 'Dynamic', a one or two berth camper based on the Doblo multi-purpose vehicle, and the 2.0 or 2.3 litre Sunchaser and Spacecruiser, the former being a high top and the latter having an elevating roof. Each are fitted with two single beds, rear bathroom and kitchen area. Both Fiats and Renaults are panel van conversions, the latter being based on the Trafic model with a choice of short or long wheelbase and either high top or raised roof to produce a compact and versatile motorhome.

There are 52 weeks in the year and as we want you to get the maximum possible use and enjoyment out of your 'Danbury' during the year... certain things are essential! You must be able to travel in complete comfort, capable of cooking, dining, washing-up easily and finally be able to set out whichever sleeping accommodation you wish... quickly and simply.

*Danbury marketing brochure 1969.
Collection of Malcolm Bobbitt.*

Fiat Amigo

Late 1970s / Italy

*Fiat Amigo marketing brochure, 1978.
Collection of Robin Hudson.*

"Easy, Easy, Easy" assured the sales patter in Amigo's publicity material: estate car sized, the motorhome was easy to handle, simple to park and equally effortless to garage.

When Fiat launched its compact 900T Small Bus (its ancestry being traced to the 1965 850 Station Wagon) at the 1976 Turin Motor Show it became an instant success. Half a million units were sold before the model was modified for 1980. Both the 900T and 900E that replaced it were converted to become some of Italy's favourite motorhomes and were produced until 1985.

With its 903 cc water-cooled rear-engine layout similar to that of Volkswagen, the little Fiat offered motorhome converters considerable scope when it came to interior style. Few conversion specialists were as successful with their designs as Isle of Man Motor Caravan Conversions who marketed the chic Amigo. "Easy, Easy, Easy" assured the sales patter in Amigo's publicity material: estate car sized, the motorhome was easy to handle, simple to park and equally effortless to garage.

The Amigo's marketing message was the vehicle's efficient use of space, and one could easily believe contemporary advertising which suggested there to be substantially more roominess than was actually the case. Seating converting to beds slept a family of five—but only when the folding berths built into the elevating roof accommodated three not-so-very-big children. The Amigo offered luxury camping with a galley that doubled as a washroom, the water container neatly located beneath the vehicle.

Fiat Amigo marketing brochure, 1978.
Collection of Robin Hudson.

Fiat amigo

The incomparable Spacemaker caravan

Left: Fiat Amigo interior from 1978 marketing brochure.
Collection of Robin Hudson.

Bottom: Fiat 600D markting brochure, mid 1950s.
Collection of Kate Trant.

Fiat 600D

Mid 1950s / Italy

Alongside the standard saloon and convertible, the first Fiat Multipla was part of the Fiat 600 range.

Left: Fiat 600D interior, mid 1950s.
Collection of the Register of
Unusual Microcars.

Bottom: Fiat 600D markting brochure,
mid 1950s.
Collection of Kate Trant.

*Bottom: Ford marketing brochure 1971.
Collection of Martin Watts/Classic Camper Club.*

SHERPA TENSING

SIR FRANCIS CHICHESTER

EDWIN E. ALDRIN

Mr & Mrs BILL JOHNSTONE & KIDS

They went places.

Ford

Think vans and commercials, and the Ford Transit occupies pole position. When Ford replaced the Thames series of models in 1965, the firm probably had little indication that 40 years later the Transit would still be in production, albeit seriously modified.

The Transit's shape and concept was ideally suited to the motorhome industry, as the vehicle offered a versatile chassis on which to build a varied number of body styles. Raised and elevating roofs, sliding doors, lift-up rear doors onto which a tent or awning could be attached: anything was possible.

Among the first motorhome producers to adopt the Transit was Sprite, followed by Bluebird, Holdsworth, Canterbury and Dormobile. Using the Transit to its full potential allowed designers to specify a complete range of motorhomes, from those affording the utmost luxury and spaciousness to six-berthers with their innovative space-saving features.

Made to measure, for years of caravanning pleasure!

The Transit proved to be a popular choice among do-it-yourself converters, many vehicles seeing long and excellent service. There was also the choice of diesel engines which afforded fuel economy, rather than petrol engines which, for motorhome use, could prove relatively expensive to run. Older motorhomes still in regular use are just as likely to be Transits than any other chassis, and therefore have become classics in their own right. Today the Transit with a choice of 2.0, 2.3 and 2.8 litre turbo diesel engines is still a popular choice among motorhome converters, their numbers including Auto-Sleepers, Chausson, Hobby, Hymermobil, Knaus, Laika, Lunar, Rapido, Swift, Timberland and Trigano.

Make space while the sun shines.

Once-a-year holidays are a thing of the past when you own a Transit motorised caravan. When you and your family can find time to get away for a few days—off you go!

1971 versions of the Canterbury Savannah Mark II, based on the Ford Transit (top) and the Canterbury Siesta, based on the Ford Escort van (bottom).
Collection of Kate Trant.

Right: Contemporary Ford Transit.

Holiday Rambler Vacationer

Contemporary / USA

At Holiday Rambler, we believe that just because you prefer the convenience and affordability of a gas motorhome, it doesn't mean you have to scrimp on luxury.

Though the Vacationer's exterior dimensions are vast, the design of the interior is cosy and comfortable. Buyers can more or less create their own vehicle from a number of layout and interior options; a range of double and triple slide-out floorplans is available in various colours and fabric combinations. Vehicles have gel coat fiberglass walls as standard and full body paint.

The design of the cockpit looks after both co-pilot and driver, with a tilting steering wheel, cruise control and a compass with outside temperature readings for the driver, and a workstation in the dashboard for the co-pilot. Taking care of safety is clearly of great importance for drivers of such large vehicles (in this case between 35 and 37 feet long).

Holiday Rambler Vacationer.
Courtesy of Holiday Rambler.

An option on the Vacationer is a three-camera rear vision system so that the driver is aware of what is behind; audio means instructions from outside the vehicle can be heard.

A hallmark of Holiday Rambler, now 51 years old, is the pride it takes in its customer care. Holiday Rambler owners become a part of Family Advantage, a support programme that includes roadside assistance and access to 350 service centres across America.

Holiday Rambler Vacationer interior.
Courtesy Holiday Rambler.

Hymer S-Class

Early 1970s / Contemporary / Germany

In Germany, the Hymer brand name has emerged as a product standard, much the same way as mechanical diggers have become known as JCBs. The first caravans to bear the Hymer name appeared in the 1930s, and the firm's Eriba range was launched in 1958. The move towards motorhome production was made in 1972, and today Hymer is a market leader in luxury motorised caravans.

With such luxury, who would want to return home?

Hymermobil 620, mid 1970s.
Courtesy Hymer AG.

When it was introduced in 2001, the S-Class, which remains in production, afforded total comfort, something that is retained for current production. The base vehicle on which the S-Class is built is Mercedes' acclaimed Sprinter with its five cylinder 2.7 litre turbo diesel engine which affords the smoothest and most refined power. Three models are offered, the shortest being a little under 22 feet, a mid size version at 25 feet, and a stretched model nearing 27 ½ feet.

HYMER

Bottom left: Hymer S class interior.
Courtesy Hymer AG.

Top: Hymermobil 900, late 1970s.
Courtesy Hymer AG.

Middle: Hymer T class interior.
Courtesy Hymer AG.

Bottom right: Hymer S class interior.
Courtesy Hymer AG.

Hymer continued...

Hymer motorhomes are built to last, and this can be appreciated by the quality of furnishings, fittings and general equipment. Take, for instance, the high-back swivel cab seats that become part of the lounge arrangement, the washroom befitting a luxury apartment, and fully equipped galley. This is the motorhome that boasts more facilities than many a city apartment, and within its not-so-restricted confines can be found a dishwasher, huge fridge/freezer and generously sized cooker. With such luxury, who would want to return home?

Hymer S820, 2004.
Courtesy Hymer AG.

Knaus Traveller

Contemporary / Germany

When it comes to being a home on wheels, the Knaus Traveller does it with panache and style. Like a lot of larger and exclusive motorhomes, the Traveller is built on Fiat's Ducato Maxi chassis. Roof-rack, ladder and anything else essential to the modern motorhome, the Traveller has it, and there is more including a garage in which to store bicycles and outdoor furniture. Compared to some motorhomes of similar size which have payloads around 400 to 500 kg, that of the Traveller's is generous at 600 kg.

A little more than 23 feet in length, 7 ½ feet in width and a fraction above 10 feet in height, the Traveller is no compact motorhome. Designed for the larger family, or a couple wanting plenty of space, this nomad is a full six-berther. Double beds are located in the spacious above-cab and over-garage compartments, as well as in the central area which converts to a dinette.

If being away from home usually means sacrificing such luxuries as a fully-fitted kitchen, bathroom and separate shower room, not to mention a compromise in day-time furnishings, the Knaus Traveller set new standards when introduced in 2002. With all the latest technology to be found on a luxury motor vehicle, the Traveller is also satisfying to drive.

Knaus Traveller rear view.
Courtesy of Knaus.

Moto-Caravan

Mid 1950s / UK

Moto-Caravans were supplied by Kent coachbuilder Peter Pitt from 1956 and boasted a choice of no fewer than 30 interior layouts, all of which were based on a variety of vehicles including Volkswagen's Kombi Transporter, Ford Thames, Commer and Austin.

The Moto-Caravan's layout versatility was a popular selling point. Space-saving designs were achieved by the use of modular furniture, and by innovatively housing cooking and washing facilities within the vehicles' interior side-door panels. Every inch of usable space was carefully considered, even to provision of fold-away bunks in the cab and at raised level in the body of the vehicle. A range of elevating roofs and awnings could be specified, the most bizarre being a loft conversion. When in the raised position, the loft was in essence a self-contained tent secured to the motorhome's roof rack.

Pitt's designs were visionary and his motorhomes were among the first to adopt high top roofs made from GRP which, when fitted, allowed in excess of six feet interior standing height. Sophistication was afforded in the style of oak-finished furnishings complete with Formica work tops, and for those owners wanting absolute luxury there was provision of a cocktail cabinet. When Peter Pitt was taken over by Canterbury Sidecars in the mid 1960s, the firm's motorhomes continued in production and were marketed as Canterbury Moto-Homes.

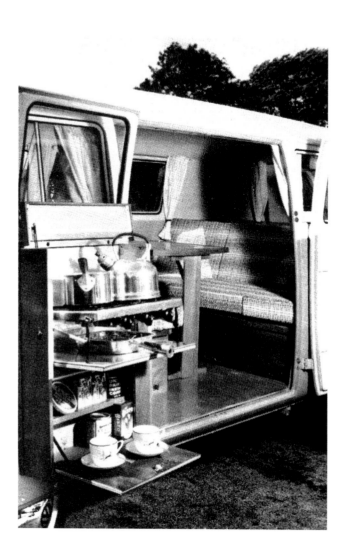

Top: Moto-Caravan marketing brochure 1963. Collection of Malcolm Bobbitt.

Bottom: Peter Pitt Moto-Caravan pictured by Harry Cook in the late 1960s. Collection of Malcolm Bobbitt.

Opposite, top: Ford 1961 'Holiday Adventurers' marketing brochure showing Moto-Caravan based on Ford Thames van. Collection of Kate Trant.

Opposite, bottom left and right: Moto-Caravan marketing brochure 1963. Collection of Malcolm Bobbitt.

The Caravan designed by PITT

For long fast journeys or short trips to town, for shopping, taking the children to school, for a conference on site, or for carrying bulky belongings, for a picnic, a week end or a holiday — the comfort and versatility of the "OPEN PLAN" combines with the dependability and manoeuvrability of the Volkswagen to create a truly outstanding all-purpose car easy for the wife to drive.

National RV Tropi-cal

Contemporary / USA

The 2005 Tropi-cal is more than just a great luxury diesel motorhome. It's a statement of who you are. It's built for fun and adventure. It's comfortable yet always functional. It exudes elegance without pretence.

National RV opened for business in 1964, initially as the Dolphin Camper Company producing a range of smaller motorhomes. The company gradually moved into the larger vehicle sector, introducing the Tropi-cal, a luxury diesel, to the market in 1996. From 35 to 39 feet in length, both interior and exterior use high quality materials and high specification technology. The LX is the top of the range Tropi-cal with the full complement of luxury features, including "lustrous full body paint", high quality computer and entertainment facilities, and "a kitchen fit for a gourmet". Focusing on the seating, instruments and vision, the Tropi-cal's driver cockpit aims to provide the most comfortable and enjoyable driving environment for long days behind the wheel. Three slide-outs extend the space and, overall, the interior design expresses a level of opulence associated with comfortable living on the move.

Bottom: National RV Tropi-cal.
Courtesy National RV.

Opposite: National RV Tropi-cal, interior.
Courtesy National RV.

National RV pride themselves on their high quality attention to detail, with thoughtful design features and high quality materials and fittings. As with most contemporary motorhome manufacturers, both large and small, customer care is key and buying a Tropi-cal means becoming a member of the National RV family, benefiting from local and national club rallies and functions, as well as the more conventional after-sales service.

Niesmann+Bischoff ClouLINER

Contemporary / Germany

At between nine and 11 yards in length, the newest range of ClouLINER motorhomes is its third generation.

Previous versions of the ClouLINER were already elegantly styled; removing the 'kink' in the roof, a characteristic feature of the previous models, has added to the already relatively clean lines of the range. Exterior storage allows bulky luggage to be stowed away while the integration of the windscreen and the front and rear lights into the body of the vehicle maintains the uncluttered design. The ClouLINER's interior layout maximises the space available as well as giving a feeling of spaciousness. The customer can choose the exterior colour, as well as the interior materials and, for an extra charge, it is even possible to specify a natural stone floor and floor heating.

At the top of the range, luxury features abound: the awning is almost invisible when not required, the rear double bed can move up and down electrically by up to 17 inches, while the main door is now remote controlled and has double locking.

The ClouLINER is always a treat for lovers of electronic gadgets. The latest models use state of the art technology both in construction and in-vehicle entertainment, including flat screen viewing with Dolby surround sound.

Opposite: ClouLINER interior.
Courtesy Niesmann+Bischoff.

Top: ClouLINER interior.
Courtesy Niesmann+Bischoff.

Bottom: ClouLINER full view.
Courtesy Niesmann+Bischoff.

Rapido

Contemporary France

The French have always been innovative when it comes to taking to the open road. Rapido, originally known for its folding caravans, offers a comprehensive range of vehicles with a choice of chassis inlcuding the Fiat Ducato or Mercedes' Sprinter. With vehicle lengths ranging from a little more than 18 feet to nearly 22 feet, the manufacturer has striven to produce motorhomes for all budgets and requirements.

Unlike a number of motorhomes which specify raised roofs, those typically designed for the French market are mostly low-profile types. Regardless, every inch of interior space is used to good effect to produce stylish living quarters employing the utmost luxury. While certain models feature shower rooms separate to washrooms, standard luxuries include clothes drying facilities, warm-air heating and stylish kitchens. Chic French mode extends to furnishings and fittings to the extent there is a holder for that essential necessity, the baguette.

Romahome

Late 1970s / Contemporary / UK & France

The first Romahome was produced in 1977. After Island Plastics bought the design, a range of models and variations followed, from demountables to coach-built vans. Base vehicles have included the Honda 545 cc Acty, the Daihatsu 850 cc (followed later by the Daihatsu 1300 cc) and the 797 cc Suzuki ST90K. The Romahome Hytop, for example, at just 15 feet 6 inches in length is one of the most compact of motorhomes. Introduced in the early 1990s and based on Citroën's small C15 van chassis, it is a two-berth Romahome powered by a 1.7 litre diesel engine. Not only is it ultra-economical, its car-like dimensions ensure that it will fit into supermarket parking spaces with ease.

We started from scratch.....
....and came up with the simple answer.

Top: Romahome marketing brochure, late 1970s.
Collection of Martin Watts/Classic Camper Club.

Left: Romahome on a Daihatsu base.
Collection of Steve Pepper/international Register of Microcaravans.

Sportsmobile

Early 1960s / Contemporary / USA

The American Sportsmobile has been around since 1961 when the VW Split Screen Transporter was adapted as a motorhome. Today Sportsmobiles take the form of motorhome conversions on such sports utility vehicles (SUVs) as Ford, Chevrolet, Dodge and Mercedes and can be delivered with regular or extended bodies, customised interiors, fixed or elevating roofs, two or four wheel drive, and a choice of petrol or diesel engines.

Sportsmobile claim that their vehicles are more than just a luxury for occasional use and are practical for everyday transportation. Being more car-sized than most motorhomes, they are easy to park, comfortable to drive and are as much at home on city streets as on rural roads: they will also fit in a garage.

Sportsmobile take care to install all water pipes inside the vehicle rather than underneath it to avoid freezing in winter; likewise air conditioning is provided by Sportsmobile's own patented Starcool system.

Top: Sportsmobile marketing
brochure, 1960s.
Courtesy Sportsmobile.

Bottom: Sportsmobile marketing
brochure, 1967.
Courtesy Sportsmobile.

Opposite: Sportsmobile marketing
brochure, 1967.
Courtesy Sportsmobile.

SNAP IN
OR OUT
FURNISHINGS
TO FIT
YOUR FUN
AND FAMILY
NEEDS

Sportsmobile

THE "FAMILY WAGON" CAMPER

FAMILY WAGON · CAMPER · UTILITY WAGON

Switch from one to the other in less than a minute—arrange furnishings to fit your activities. Luxurious styling, highest quality material and craftsmanship assure maintenance-free year-round enjoyment. Optional Pop Top snaps up in a second to catch the slightest breeze. Free-standing canopy and side walls accessories add a room in minutes, to hold your campsite or to enjoy at home. Canopy top may be left off for a private sunroom or solarium. Side-walls have sewn in nylon floor.

Suntrekker

Early 1970s / UK

Though not a new idea, the concept of the dismountable motorhome became popular in the autumn of 1973 with the emergence of the Suntrekker at the London Caravan Show. Suntrekker attracted a lot of attention, for it was a hybrid, and a successful one at that, remaining in production until 1989.

In what was in theory a simple idea, Suntrekker mirrored the American theme to produce a mobile home that could be easily and conveniently loaded and unloaded from a pick-up truck, often a Bedford or Ford Transit. It seemed a good idea to be able to drive to a camping site and deposit the motorhome body, thus allowing the pick-up vehicle to be used for touring purposes.

Suntrekker marketing brochures.
Collection of Martin Watts/
Classic Camper Club.

Opposite, from top to bottom:
Suntrekker (Leyland Sherpa),
Suntrekker (Mercedes L306D)
and Suntrekker (Bedford C F).
Collection of Martin Watts/
Classic Camper Club.

Mounting and de-mounting the mobile camper worked well enough, though the operation required some precision. De-mounting meant that the camper had to be jacked to clear the pick-up base before being supported on the ground using retractable stilts. Mounting it aboard the vehicle demanded some deft navigation on behalf of the driver, but with practice was a straightforward procedure.

The Suntrekker's specification was such that it included a refrigerator, cooker, toilet compartment and optional shower. Provision was made for a bunk bed in the forward elevated compartment, while the dinette could be converted to sleeping quarters.

Toyota Hi-Ace

Early 1970s / Japan

Before the explosive arrival of Japanese vehicles onto the British and European markets, the motorhome industry was largely structured around Volkswagen, BMC, Bedford, Commer and Ford. With its 1.6 litre Hi-Ace model introduced in 1972, Toyota sought to supply chassis to motorhome manufacturers.

Ci Caravans were first to adopt the Hi-Ace chassis, and thereafter Toyota took greater hold on the motorhome market, especially as Volkswagen allowed only approved converters to use its name and products without invalidating the firm's warranty.

Hi-Ace marketing brochure.
Collection of Martin Watts/
Classic Camper Club.

Hi-Ace marketing brochure.
Collection of the Dormobile Owners Club.

Another well known name to adopt the Toyota chassis was Dormobile whose new model for 1973, the New World, was compact, good looking and well specified; the raised roof substantially increasing the vehicle's interior accommodation. That is where the plus points ended owing to dubious handling. The New World's height and short wheelbase made stability on motorways dire, especially in side-winds and when being overtaken by juggernauts. Adding insult to injury, its cost, in excess of £2,000, was high.

Reviews of the New World were non-complimentary; customers complained; sales were miserable and within two years the model was dropped from the catalogue. As for the Toyota chassis, it continued in production with acclaim, courtesy of a number of manufacturers including Devon, Glendale, Multicruiser and Newlander.

The Lite-Ace is the Hi-Ace's smaller sibling and dates from 1990. It is indeed small at a little over 12 feet in length, and is in reality a single-berth motorhome that can accommodate two people with some cosiness. A panel van conversion, the Lite-Ace was used by a number of specialist converters: it has a 1.5 litre petrol engine mated to a five-speed gearbox and does not have the sophistication of power steering. More car-like than a purpose-built motorhome, the Lite-Ace does have an elevating roof, and access to the vehicle interior is via a side-opening door, though there is a tailgate which gives access to minimal storage facilities. Access from the cab through to the rear compartment is denied because the engine is located between and beneath the two cab seats.

The Lite-Ace interior has a bench seat which converts to a bed; there is a small sink and a hob is mounted on top of a tiny refrigerator. Other features include a water container, folding table and space for a gas bottle. Whilst not in the same league as other compact motorhomes it nevertheless affords a level of basic accommodation which might be convenient for short periods on the move.

Top: New World Toyota marketing brochure, 1973.
Collection of the Dormobile Owners Club.

Opposite: Toyota Lite-Ace, early 1990s.
Collection of the Dormobile Owners Club.

Volkswagen Transporter

Early 1950s / Contemporary / Germany

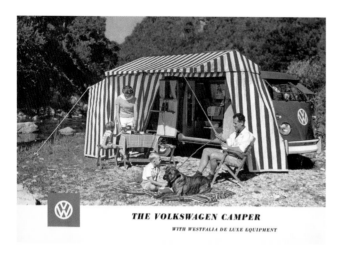

*1960 Westfalia marketing brochure.
Collection of Everett Barnes.*

With its robust box-like structure, its hardy Beetle-derived air-cooled drive train neatly positioned out of the way within its tail, Volkswagen's Type 2 Transporter effectively kick-started the postwar motorhome industry. The first caravan manufacturer to recognise the Volkswagen's qualities was the German firm Westfalia, which introduced the Camping Box in 1951. Within eight years Westfalia had built 1,000 Camping Boxes and, by 1969, 50,000.

The Westfalia's interior design was without equal. By day it afforded every facility to include a dining area with folding tables, kitchen with running water and plentiful cupboard space in which to store all that was needed for a camping holiday. At night the table and seats almost magically converted into a double and two children's beds, and raising the concertina-style roof canopy aided ventilation while adding to the vehicle's interior spaciousness.

On the road, the Volkswagen's air-cooled engine was impervious to climate conditions, seldom freezing in winter nor over-heating in summer. The vehicle's deft design with its space-saving characteristics, double side doors and optional awning, emerged as a model which other motorhome suppliers strove to emulate.

Not so much a vehicle... more a way of life.

Devon Motor Caravans 1979.

A premier British motorhome supplier of the postwar era, Lisburne Garage of Torquay marketed the Devon range of VW conversions in association with Sidmouth-based cabinet maker J P White. Lisburne's first offering was based on a standard 1131 cc air-cooled VW Transporter, the only external alteration being a side awning which attached to the roof of the vehicle, and which was available in several styles and sizes.

Two versions of the Devon were offered. For a little under £900 (equivalent today to £23,000), one could buy the basic model which accommodated two adults, while a further £10 (£250) afforded the de luxe with two additional children's beds, one in the cab and the other positioned above the engine compartment.

The Devon's interior arrangement was simple, though spartan by today's standards. In the centre of the vehicle, a dinette comprised two couches and Formica covered tables, which, when folded, converted to a double bed. Cupboard units provided useful storage space and housed a built-in calor gas cooker. The de luxe model additionally featured the luxury of a refrigerator and washbasin, the extra price outlay offering good value for money. For families wanting a camping holiday with a difference, the Devon offered no end of opportunities.

A hard working Devon motor caravan earns its holidays in the sun.

Devon marketing brochure.
Collection of Malcolm Bobbitt.

When coachbuilder Martin Walter of Folkestone in Kent introduced its Transporter based Dormobile in 1954, the Transporter's engine size had been increased to 1192 cc to provide a 25 per cent power boost. During the same year Volkswagen produced its 100,000th "brick on wheels". One of the Dormobile's outstanding features was its elevating roof. In addition to the feeling of increased spaciousness, the roof, when in the raised position, allowed sufficient height for occupants to stand upright and move around the vehicle in comfort. Another advantage was that fold-away bunks fitted at roof level could accommodate a couple of adults or children when the canopy was raised, the means of access to the upper bunks being a folding step ladder.

The Dormobile's 'Dormatic seating' was a further characteristic. In easy movements the seats could be folded to a double bed or two separate bunks, or when the need arose, to be stowed against the vehicle's wall in order to maximise floor space. Other Dormobile specifications included curtains, fluorescent lighting, a wardrobe, calor gas cooking and water supply pumped from an on-board container.

Take a Volkswagen Kombi, add the famous Dormobile roof, build in the de luxe Dormobile cupboards, wardrobe, sink units and water pump, hide away the big cooker, carefully fit the unique cool box, hand the colourful curtains, match the deep cushioned upholstery, make the beds, fold up the bunks, and you've got.... A VOLKSWAGEN DORMOBILE MOTOR CARAVAN.

You Will Have

NO HOTEL WORRIES
CATERING PROBLEMS
COSTLY TRAVEL
LOST TIME
PURCHASE TAX
TOWING PROBLEMS
THERE IS NOTHING TO TOW !

with the CARAVETTE

LICENSED AS A PRIVATE CAR—ANNUAL ROAD TAX £12 10 0

Devon Caravette marketing brochure.
Collection of Malcolm Bobbitt.

Dormobile marketing brochure, late 1960s.
Collection of Malcolm Bobbitt.

The Volkswagen caravan

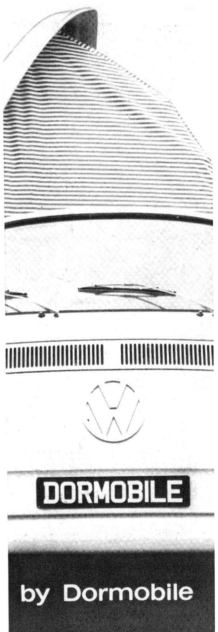

DORMOBILE

by Dormobile

Winnebago

Mid 1960s / Contemporary / USA

In motorhome parlance the American Winnebago name has largely come to identify any of the leviathans, some to be seen with a car in tow, which have become an increasingly familiar sight on European roads. In North America, the Winnebago is a way of life, offering truly a home away from home.

Arguably the motorhome of all motorhomes, the Winnebago Brave is the long-running model to have emerged from one of America's premier motorised caravan constructors. The Brave was introduced in 1971 and built on the 5 litre Dodge M300 petrol-engined chassis incorporating three-speed automatic transmission as standard. Demure by modern Winnebago standards, the Brave when introduced was a mere 18 ¼ feet in length and 7 ½ feet wide.

Winnebago Brave, 2003.
Courtesy Winnebago Industries, Inc.

Though retired in 2004, today the Brave is considered by some to be the ultimate motorhome and is ideal when it comes to touring America's expansive landmass. Taken for granted are features such as air-conditioning and central heating; larger models incorporate a slide-out arrangement which, when the vehicle is moored on a camping site, substantially increases the vehicle's interior space. In addition to sumptuous furnishings, Winnebagos come complete with beds and bathrooms of a size which would embarrass many a hotel.

Propelling the Brave is a 6.5 litre turbo diesel Chevrolet or Workhorse engine according to specification with four-speed automatic transmission and power steering. Fuel economy is hardly an issue here, but even so by today's standards is heavy when compared to more modern vehicles. Manoeuvrability on all but the widest and straightest highways calls for some deft navigational skills, but this is but a small price to pay for a palace on wheels which has, as part of its specification, a built-in generator, hydraulic steadies for firm ground anchorage, roll-out awning and solar panels.

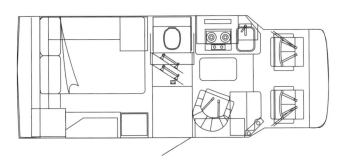

Top left: Winnebago Rialta interior layout.

Top right: Winnebago Rialta kitchen.

Bottom: Winnebago Rialta full view.
Courtesy Winnebago Industries, Inc.

Winnebago continued...

Substantially smaller than its larger sibling, the Winnebago Rialta is still impressive compared to European standards. When introduced in the mid 1990s the Rialta was built on the Volkswagen T4 chassis, and with its five cylinder 2.5 litre petrol engine, the vehicle is more akin to American usage in terms of fuel economy. Transmission is courtesy of a four-speed gearbox and naturally there is power steering.

Despite the Rialta's dimensions, 21 foot long and 7 foot 4 inches wide, it is only a two-berth motorhome, and this is sufficient to illustrate the amount of interior spaciousness that is available. With the accent on comfort, the cab seats swivel to form a dinette-cum-lounge with a central galley. Amidships is the washroom with its separate shower and toilet, all of which makes efficient use of space. Luxury accessories include a solar panel for water heating, air conditioning, awning and a bike rack.

Winnebago Adventurer, 2005.
Courtesy Winnebago Industries, Inc.

Chapter Four

Compact Living

Kate Trant

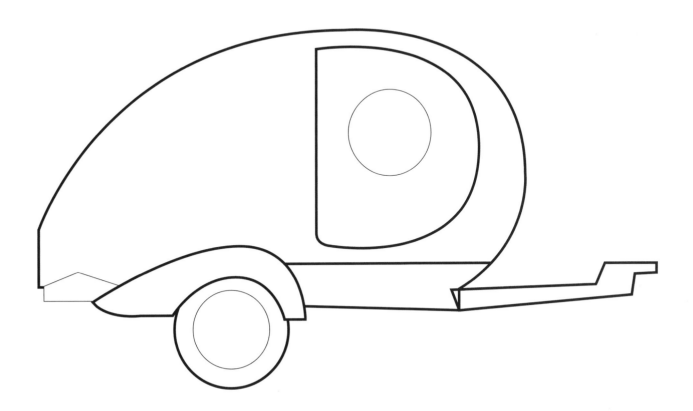

Design and mobility

You just have to be minimal.

Gaynor and Graham Stevens.

In the late 1970s, architect Alison Smithson stated: "it's not that caravans are bad housing… but that most housing isn't as good as caravans". She was referring to the Airstream, which, though one of the most potent icons of modern mobile living, is neither necessarily the 'van of choice for most, nor the most economically available; nonetheless implicit here is a celebration of the high quality design that Airstream represents, for enthusiast and design cognoscenti alike. Early Airstreams, with their uncompromising design aesthetic, have become both benchmark and inspiration, fundamentally related to yet set apart from their mobile cousins. The Airstream, like the VW bus, is one of a curiously small number of designed objects that elicits admiration from design connoisseur and enthusiast alike, causing many a sharp intake of breath on the very rare sightings outside the confines of a dedicated rally. Its shiny aluminium exterior shell and beautifully appointed interior now represents one of the highest standards for the design of small as well as mobile spaces, both in terms of construction standards and, crucially, in terms of aesthetics. Other makes and models come close in terms of their optimum use of available space but few yet rival it for looks.

WBCCI Hobo Rally, Blythe, California, USA. February 2001.
Photograph by Jenny Nordquist.

A place for everything and everything in its place

It's all about getting a quart into a pint pot.

Terry Martin.

How do you get the outside round the inside?

Doctor Who.[1]

Designing small is just as valid a pursuit as designing big. In fact the challenges faced by the designer in working with smaller spaces which they have to use both economically and creatively are arguably greater than those where space is not at a premium. As Terence Conran put it in *Small Spaces*, "The first step in thinking 'small' is to think positive. The high market value of space has a tendency to reinforce the view that a small area is necessarily substandard, second best." Of course, at 40 foot long and more, the Americans at the larger end of the motorhome spectrum rival some contemporary urban homes in terms of square footage. However, it is the combination of size and mobility that makes the design of these vehicles so interesting—their ability to bring together in a defined space what is required to live life on the road. When it comes to optimising space, some of the most creative and ingenious solutions can be seen in the design of motorhomes and camper vans. Part of the designer's brief is to create spaces that are easy for owners to maintain and manage, and a range of floorplans and inventive products and fittings have developed over time specifically for this market. Designs have to make the most of every last inch of space while devices such as extending roofs and slide-outs provide additional temporary floorspace or head height on site.

Optional Equipment **Tent** 7' x 8' sturdy nylon with vinyl floor. External aluminum frame for easy set-up. Zippered door, screened windows. Connecting boot to camper. Firmly free-standing.

other VW Camping Ideas . . . .

A free-standing tent for Squarebacks!
Adapted for use with the VW Squareback, the large, sturdy tent has all the features of the Camper tent—plus a special boot that makes it a snug "extension" of your car. Easy to carry and set up.

This page and overleaf: A range of solutions to the problem of limited space.

Top right: Courtesy Holiday Rambler.

Top left, middle right and bottom: Collection of Malcolm Bobbitt.

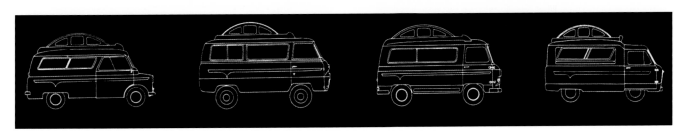

Home comforts
on four wheels in the luxurious
COMMER CARAVAN
PETROL OR DIESEL

Top:
Collection of Martin Watts/
Classic Camper Club.

Bottom: National RV Tropi-cal.
Courtesy National RV.

"The best way to design the inside of your bus is to live in it for a while and see how the flow of people and movement and storage works best—and by the time you get down to it... it falls into place."[2]

The design of many of the early motorhomes more or less set the model for what was to follow and, in many ways, little has changed. Decisions relating to the organisation of the interior have, for example, revolved around the size and relative position of the kitchen or dinette in relation to other living areas and the type and location of beds and how they function. On the face of it, the repertoire as it stands is relatively fixed, constrained as it is within a range of dimensions that are embedded in legislation. It would appear that all that is up for grabs are minor changes in floorplans and the best use of new technology. But, as with any design practice, this is seldom the case and the good designer will bring to the table a range of sophisticated skills and technical knowledge as well as a range of styling cues that offer a design language that is as deep as it is wide. What this achieves is not a range of superficial add-ons for the sake of sales and marketing but careful and considered use of a contemporary design language aimed at specific market sectors.

A number of small-scale manufacturers are producing more or less bespoke interiors for existing vehicles, much as has always been done in the motorhome fraternity, along the lines of 'self-build'. However, this is not necessarily a cheap way to get the van of your dreams and a market is building to cater for those who do not necessarily have the skills or the time to 'do it themselves' but want something smart and cool. Some manufacturers are now producing ultra small caravans that also appeal to a style conscious audience, such as the T@B.

If there's one thing missing from some contemporary motorhomes, it's character.

Motorhome, March 2005.

As with the mainstream automotive industry, as the motorhome sector developed, vehicles on the market became harder and harder to differentiate so that, to the inexperienced eye, the contemporary landscape is populated with either a host of white 'Europeans' with little apart from internal specifications, fabrics and layouts to distinguish one from another, or a range of huge 'Americans' with similarly undistinguishable characteristics. Only a change of context— an American in Europe, a vintage vehicle on a motorway, highway or autoroute, or a particularly personal self-build or conversion, is likely to bring comment from an outsider.

The T@B.
Photograph with permission from
Cequent Products, Inc. and Dutchmen
Manufacturing, Inc.

Currently there are few real examples of a contemporary design language in the motorhome and camper sector. As in the automotive industry as a whole, it is easy to glance fondly backwards at a time when apparently not every motorhome looked the same as every other. But the manufacturing stakes are high and not to be taken lightly. In the contemporary motorhome and camper van market, the addition of a larger pre-retirement population to the existing ownership offers rich pickings and requires the development of a correspondingly youthful design language.

It is more and more commonly acknowledged that, in general in the UK and Europe, the older proportion of the population is growing. "Over the next 25 years in Britain, the number of people aged 45 to 64 years will increase by 3 ½ million. Across Europe the figure will be 20 million."[3] These particular statistics, from The Future Foundation, are supported by the projections of other research bodies. And it is not simply the numbers themselves that are important but the types of individuals they describe. "Consider a woman born in England in 1950. She might have gone shopping in Carnaby Street in the late 1960s, [had] demonstrated against the Vietnam War in 1968 and seen Jimi Hendrix play at the Isle of Wight festival two years later." Given general patterns of childbearing over the next four or so decades, by 2005, "Our swinging sixties rebel" is "55 years old and a grandparent".[4]

In the USA meanwhile, the RVIA's 2005 Business Indicators show that the already blooming 55 and over market is expanding but that this market sector is also growing to embrace a younger age group, with buyers aged 35 to 54 being the largest and fastest-growing segment of the RV market. Overall, the number of RVing households in the USA is estimated to rise by 15 per cent during 2001 to 2010 to nearly eight million.

Every day, 11,000 Americans turn 50.

Contemporary European motorhome design
solutions.

Opposite top and bottom:
Courtesy Dethleffs.

Opposite bottom and left: Courtesy Knaus.

Camper van and motorhome use appeals to a diverse audience. Where for the time being the assumption might prevail that it is predominantly the territory of the retired couple, it in fact crosses both economic and generational boundaries. On the roads of Europe and the USA, the sight of a couple of retirees taking the opportunity to make the most of their new-found freedom to see places and sights that the constraints of their working lives prevented them from seeing is common. Relatively common too are parents showing their young families the landmarks of Europe, while even younger couples or groups of friends enjoy the freedom of a mobile lifestyle on a tighter budget for a summer in an old VW or Mercedes bus. The interesting area for growth is coming both from the increase in size and breadth of the 'ageing' population, and the resulting expansion into what then becomes the 'younger' market. Contemporary promotional material is increasingly populated by younger couples and families as well as older couples. Increasing awareness of the environmental cost of flying and interest in holidaying 'closer to home' can only add to this popularity.

Recognising this, and in order to sustain its existing audience and appeal to a wider one, in the UK in 2005 The Caravan Club launched The Caravan of the Future, a design competition asking for ideas for the next generation of 'mobile' home.

Competition judge, caravanner and designer Wayne Hemingway explains:

> ... caravan and motorcaravan designs have not changed substantially over the years and we hope this competition will bring some innovative and environmentally friendly new designs that will reflect the modern caravanner's wants and needs.[5]

Small has become the new big.

Irene Rawlings and Mary Abel, *Portable Houses*, p. 77.

With over 500 entries from designers, architects, enthusiasts and the like at the time of writing, the competition is a clear signal from all sides—owners, industry and design fraternity—that now is a fertile period for caravan design. Far from designing for small spaces being a somehow inferior activity, this competition offers the design community in the widest sense the opportunity to demonstrate in a very public fashion that designers can apply their skills to design high quality, small spaces that optimise the available room and develop a contemporary, sophisticated design language that suits.

"... you will want to plan for accessibility, changeability and durability."[6]

We see our moving van as an apartment on wheels which every six months or so is relocated.

Roll Your Own, p. 48.

Circus Circus RV Resort, Las Vegas, Nevada, USA.
Februray 2001.
Photograph by Jenny Nordquist.

Getting away from it all

We've been in places where there just ain't any people for as far as you can see in any direction, for miles and miles and miles. They talk about it being crowded and all that. It's crowded right around New York and right around Los Angeles, it's really crowded, and not much fun. But you get out in the rest of the country and there's a lot of country left, and it ain't so bad. It's a pretty good-looking country.[7]

In *Complicated Lives*, two authors from The Future Foundation set out to describe the increasing complexity of our contemporary lives and discuss how our dissatisfaction with that complexity keeps pace. They list the overwhelming choice with which we are presented daily—the options available for orange juice, dental floss, microwave ovens, and TVs as well as TV channels. Leaving aside the complexities involved in choosing a motorhome or van from particularly complex options, owners make tough decisions about what to leave behind. Space restrictions limit possessions and the definition of 'essential' is put into clear focus when faced with choosing one possession over another. These choices apply as much to part- as to full-timers; sometimes the decisions faced by those who decide to commit completely are simply too final and many will choose to store their belongings for a while until they are sure that the full-time life is for them.

Even *Roll Your Own*, the classic guide to an alternative lifestyle in a "Truck, Bus, Van or Camper", could not leave behind all the comforts of home: "Living in a truck, school bus or a van is an alternative to living in an apartment or house. The joy, freedom and comfort of having your home and all the things you enjoy with you must be experienced to be believed."

On the one hand, many of those taking part in or tempted by the mobile lifestyle want a temporary or permanent return to a simpler existence. On the other hand, few want to leave everything behind and most speak of 'home comforts'. What this constitutes varies as much as the meaning of 'home'. For some it will mean elaborate furnishings, TV, stereo and integrated barbecue; for others fewer possessions or a more pared down aesthetic. Either way, what is required of the designer is to fulfil the expectations of as many potential owners as possible by integrating these requirements into the vehicle without losing the overall integrity of the design, interior or exterior.

Although over the decades a number of manufacturers have promoted the use of their vehicles for business, using your bus as a mobile office has not yet caught on to a great extent. However, access to technology and the resulting miniaturisation of products is making it easier to fit more facilities into a vehicle. This means that, coupled with the increased use of the internet for communication, and the introduction of Wi-Fi hotspots across many countries, pursuing business interests whilst on the move is becoming a more common occurrence amongst owners.

When you're nomadic you tend not to keep close trace of the 'day' and 'hours'.

What constitutes 'home comforts' varies as much as the meaning of 'home'. For some it will mean elaborate furnishings, TV, stereo and integrated barbecue; for others fewer possessions or a more pared down aesthetic.

Not only is a Transit caravan a mobile holiday home, it can also be used as a temporary office or for specialised business applications. Many business men have found that a Transit caravan is the complete answer to all their accommodation and transportation problems. Wherever your business takes you, even over the roughest roads and to the remotest districts, you can take your own bedroom, kitchen and office with you.

Ford Transit marketing brochure, 1966.
Collection of Kate Trant.

Of no fixed abode?: perceptions and reality

The meanings associated with campers and motorhomes across the spectrum of owners are complex: both powerful yet pointless at one and the same time. Witness the naming and renaming of the bodies representing both the mobile manufactured housing industry and trailer industry in the USA in the second half of the twentieth century in order to dodge the remarkably tenacious negative connotations associated with these forms of dwelling.[8] Old assumptions pertain, even today, but many contemporary associations are based on cultural meanings the origins of which no longer exist, or are so far in the dim and distant past as to be entirely irrelevant.

Meanings have also been confused in both the UK and the USA by debates and legislation as to what actually constitutes 'mobility' in a home, when some mobile homes have wheels but never move, some unfeasibly large homes are actually mobile, and the line between 'vehicle' and 'house' is itself somewhat portable. Many owners have been getting on with it quietly and simply for years, ignoring myth and unsubstantiated or dated prejudice, behaving in ways that contribute rather than detract from society. Today the world of the motorhome has travelled the spectrum of ownership from the fabulously rich to the utterly dispossessed and all statuses in-between. Now, travelling homes that cost as much as a house, and are better specified than many, are owned and used by people with no other home or as a second home. Smaller, simpler and far more modest vans are used by those with comfortable amounts of disposable income as a way to return, occasionally, to a simpler, more laid-back lifestyle. In the world of the camper van and motorhome at least, when it comes to gauging a person's status by the vehicle they drive and the way they live, normal rules do not necessarily apply.

Always leave a little more than you take, visible or invisible.

Roll Your Own, p. 170.

Mount Rushmore RV park, South Dakota, USA.
July 2002.
Photograph by Jenny Nordquist.

Many owners have been getting on with it quietly and simply for years.

The environmental credentials of the majority of motorhomes and camper vans are not exemplary. Fuel consumption tends to be high across the board. Many of the vehicles currently on the roads of the USA, UK and Europe and were built before we entered our current environmentally conscious era. However, progress is being made. In 1974, *Roll Your Own* advocated conversion to propane for about $300:

> If you're interested in doing something about air and water pollution now, and drive a gasoline-fuelled, internal-combustion engine vehicle, convert to propane. Conversion is a simple, financially beneficial operation which reduces your vehicle's harmful emissions by 50 per cent.[9]

By 2004, the EarthRoamer XV-LT had taken the meaning of 'self-contained' to new heights by running most of its interior systems using two solar-charged batteries meaning that it does not depend on external power or water hookups. It runs on regular diesel or biodiesel. As with the automotive industry as a whole, the more these alternative methods of power are developed, introduced and used, the more economically viable they will become. In general, there is a level of environmental awareness amongst owners who are diligent in removing all trace of their presence when moving on.

> It shouldn't be necessary to mention, but if someone is kind enough to allow you to camp on his land, be sure you clean up after yourself. Don't leave him a mess and regrets about letting you stay. This also makes it easier for the next person who might want to stay there.[10]

Everywhere you are on the planet is HOME. Take care of it, clean up after others.

The road takes you to other people's HOMES as well. They were there before you came, will be there after you leave. Learn how they do it there. People who stay in one place identify with a piece of land and are suspicious of those who move a lot.

Roll Your Own, p. 124.

One of the key requirements of most camper van and motorhome owners is to take with them all that is needed for their journey, long or short. The need to be self-contained has brought about a range of results, from the very complex needs of 'boondocking', to a far simpler set of requirements for drivers of less complex vehicles.

Outside the motorhome market, the desire and ability to become self-contained developed in earnest through the 1970s. The launch of the Sony Walkman in July 1979 marked a major landmark. The somewhat bemused reaction of the press was an indication of just how innovative this new product was. Journalists were taken to a park in Tokyo where they were given a Walkman and a pair of headphones. They were then played an explanation of the Walkman (in stereo) while Sony staff demonstrated its use on bicycles and roller skates. Of course, the Walkman caught on in a big way, becoming a springboard for a whole host of subsequent developments.

Top: Apple's contemporary answer to portable audio—the iPod.
Courtesy Apple.

Bottom left: Sony Walkman.

Bottom right: Part of the Mandarina Duck md20 range.
Courtesy Mandarina Duck.

Leaving aside the technological wizardry that made the Walkman possible, suddenly we could take our music with us wherever we went. For the duration of a set of long-life batteries we could walk or travel on bus or tube or train with little or no reference to what was going on around us. The ipod has taken us many steps further, offering even greater control by letting us choose tunes to suit our mood. Now, the true twenty-first century urbanite can carry the world on their back (in their Mandarina Duck backpack), disappear into their own world with a personalised range of music and, with the rapidly increasing number of public access Wi-Fi hotspots across the USA, UK and beyond, need no longer be tied to a conventional workplace. Increasingly, motorhome owners, especially full-timers, keep in touch with family and friends, and keep up with the latest information by accessing the internet either in libraries or at WiFi locations using their own laptops.

We've got a motorhome, we're self contained!

From Dusk Till Dawn, 1996.

At €95, the French Nabaztag is the latest gizmo on the market, a Wi-Fi rabbit that communicates a range of messages using the position of its ears and changing patterns of lights on its body.
Courtesy of Violet.

Maximum living area with minimum outer dimensions.

Whether brought about by necessity or desire, smaller spaces have become cooler through design and a look at contemporary small spaces reveals some remarkable complete and creative compact solutions.

Colani Rotor House

German developer Hanse Haus worked with designer Luigi Colani to produce the Colani Rotor House, a single-room dwelling 20 x 20 foot square. Inside is a rotating cylinder that contains, in turn, a diminutive bathroom, kitchen and bedroom. It has an open front and is remote-controlled, turning to bring to the opening whichever element is required.

Exterior of the Colani Rotor House.
Courtesy Hanse Haus.

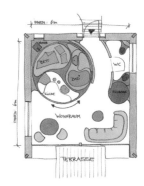

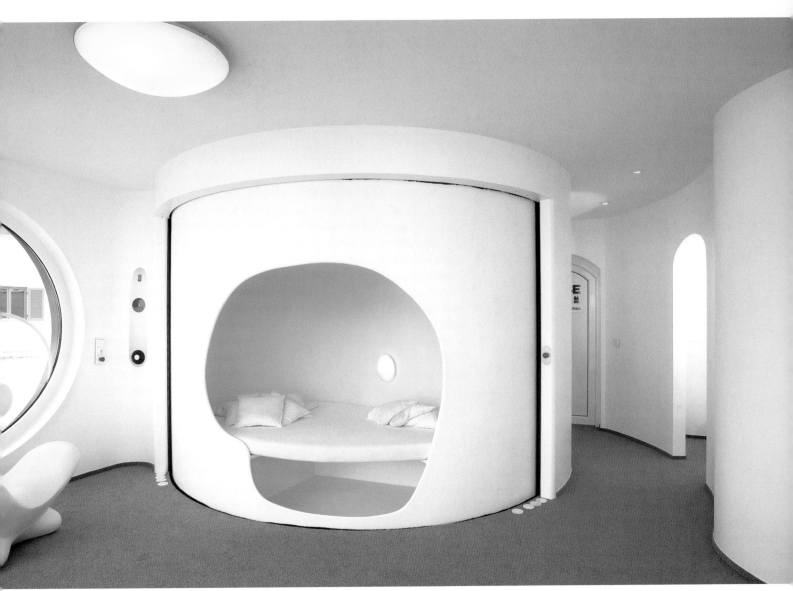

Yotel

Designed by Priestman Goode, who also worked on the Airbus 380, the inspiration for Yotel came from British Airways first class cabins and Japanese hotels. Each room, though only 11 square yards, contains a range of facilities and services. It is the use of internal windows, that look onto corridors naturally lit by reflective mechanisms and channelling light, that enable Yotels to be built on conventionally difficult sites.

Yotel would appeal to the magazine's readers, hip young urbanites. If a hotel is priced perilously low you're usually afraid of what you will find lurking behind the door. Knowing you can get a clean, crisp room with some designer panache is an attractive proposition.

Budget Living, 2004.

Top: Techno Wall.
Courtesy Yotel.

Bottom: Yotel exterior.
Courtesy Yotel.

Opposite: Yotel room.
Courtesy Yotel.

The award-winning Skybed has been designed for your comfort. With an in-built back massager and an extensive range of seat adjustments, it offers outstanding comfort in every position.

Skybed ▶

With its comforting cocoon design, a seat that extends to become a bed seven feet long, storage solutions including a place to put your shoes and the work you have brought with you on your flight, and a high quality entertainment system, the award-winning Skybed designed for Qantas by Australian designer Mark Newson contains many of the accoutrements required for a self-contained lifestyle.

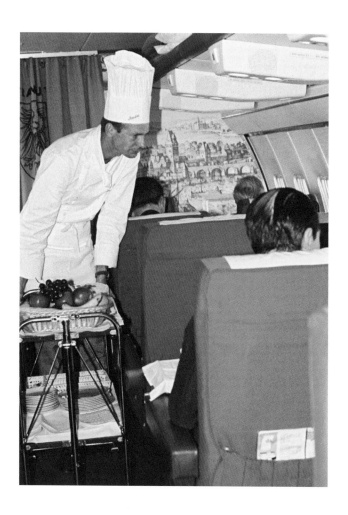

*Senator Service in a first class cabin of a
Lufthansa Boeing 707, 1965.
Courtesy Deutsche Lufthansa AG.*

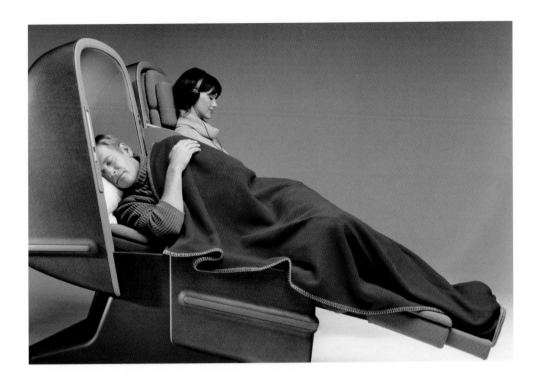

Skybed as set and extended to seven feet long.
Courtesy Marc Newson Ltd and Quantas Airways Ltd.

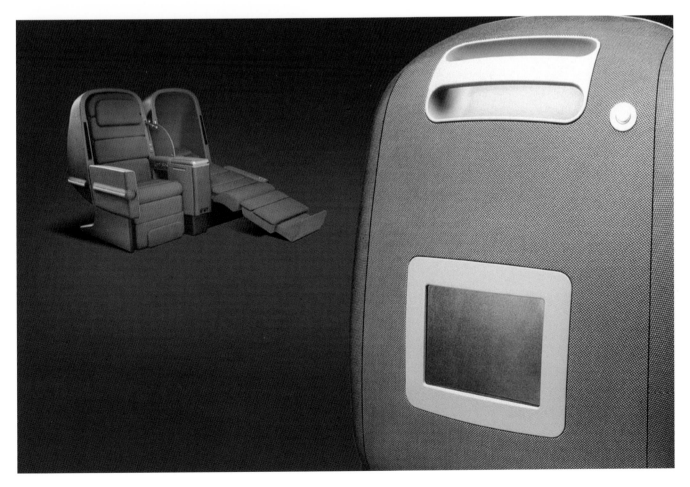

Design, motorhomes and camper vans now

Airstream Skydeck

Motorhomes with exterior decks have been in existence since the very earliest days of mobile living. However, the Airstream Skydeck takes the idea to a new level with a patio on its roof that more or less doubles the size of the vehicle and can seat 15 people. Aside from the roof deck, the Skydeck is rather fantastically appointed, with two slide-outs to increase the living area, panoramic windows and telephone hookup and home theatre system in the bedroom. The Skydeck is only available in the USA.

Courtesy of Airstream Inc.

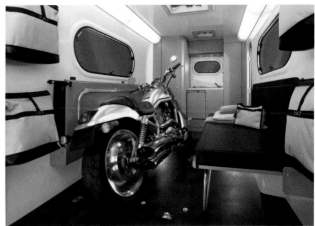

The YAT

The YAT—Young Activity Trailer—is a caravan designed for Knaus by automotive designer Peter Naumann. It is just under 18 foot long and just over seven foot wide, with an interior space just over six foot wide and just over six and a half foot high. One of few examples of a pared down aesthetic, the YAT's interior has folding tables and beds to leave room to carry motorbikes and sports equipment whilst on the road.

A caravan, whatever the funky new moniker, but a distant relative of the sheet-metal slugs that clog up slow lanes of motorways each summer.

Wallpaper*.

Volkswagen Microbus

VW has reconceived the Microbus for the twenty-first century. Launched at the 2001 Detroit Motor Show, the concept takes advantage of the vast amount of technology available on the market since the original some 50 years ago. Whilst the new Microbus offers a dynamic and exciting progression, it is unlikely that the original VW bus will ever lose its value, emotional or financial.

The Volkswagen bus was never just a means of transport, it has always been an emotive cult object. The public's reaction at motor shows combined with the findings of market studies already suggests that the Microbus design has a spontaneous appeal, and that the vehicle will follow in the footsteps of its successful predecessor.

It is not easy to live a romantic mobile lifestyle now that every stone has been turned, it is hard to go 'off the beaten track' and practically all the four corners of the earth have been visited. But the good news is that it's 'anything goes' in the world of camper vans and motorhomes; anyone can drive anything and, though on close scrutiny common themes emerge, there are almost as many reasons for living the mobile life and approaches to it as there are people living it. Assumptions may be tenacious but equally the culture in which it is possible for those assumptions to be challenged prevails and the range of owners is diverse and, in fact, contemporary US, UK and European motorhome and camper van use is about as respectable as could be. At the top end of the market, these vehicles are better equipped and cost more than many people's homes; even at the lower end, prices demand commitment and dedication. There is an ever-increasing design awareness amongst contemporary owners and, above all, there is a vibrancy and impassioned attitude amongst these owners and their families about the nature of this type of travel—independent, expansive and ambitious.

I can hardly remember when I didn't think camping. I've always had terrible gypsy feet!

Owner interviewed by Dorothy and David Counts, *Over the Next Hill,* p. 92.

Volkswagen Microbus concept, 2001.

Endnotes

1. *Doctor Who* episode, 4 June 2005. The first episode of *Doctor Who* was screened in the UK on 23 November 1963. TARDIS means "Time and Relative Dimension in Space". Its key characteristic is that its external dimensions bear little relation to what is inside it. "The interior of the TARDIS occupies a separate set of dimensions to the exterior—so it's a lot bigger on the inside than the outside. And inside there are an awful lot of rooms—libraries, gardens, swimming pools, and even a cricket pavilion." www.bbc.co.uk/cult/doctorwho/tardiscam/intro

2. Pallidini, J and Dubin, B, *Roll Your Own: The Complete Guide to Living in a Truck, Bus, Van or Camper*, Macmillan Publishing Co, Inc, 1974, p. 39.

3. Willmott, M and Nelson, W, *Complicated Lives*, The Future Foundation/John Wiley and Sons, 2003, p. 85.

4. It is important to note that the focus of *Complicated Lives* is the 70 per cent of the British population who form the 'affluent majority' rather than the proportion that is confronted by 'deprivation', rather than 'complexity'.

5. Hemingway, Wayne, *Building Design*, 17 June 2005.

6. Pallidini, and Dubin, *Roll Your Own*, p. 46.

7. Pallidini, and Dubin, *Roll Your Own*, p. 182.

8. "'Trailer' meant temporary housing for poor people. It had to go. In 1953 the Trailer Coach Manufacturers' Association became the Mobile Home Manufacturers' Association (MHMA). 20 years later, 'mobile home' had picked up its share of negative associations and name inflation demanded another denomination. In 1975 the MHMA changed its name to the Manufactured Housing Institute, removing all reference to mobility..." Davies, C, *The Prefabricated Home*, Reaktion Books, 2005, pp. 77-78.

9. Pallidini, and Dubin, *Roll Your Own*, p. 48.

10. Pallidini, and Dubin, *Roll Your Own*, p. 136.

References

Agnew, Derek. *The A-Z of Caravanning*, Barker, 1976.

Anderson, William C, *The Two-Ton Albatross, or, Across a trans-continental highway in a travel trailer with two kids, two guppies, a miniature orange tree, a lobster named Hud, a Saint Bernard dog, and a claustrophobic wife*, Crown Publishers, 1969.

Baker, Kim and Sunny, *The RVer's Bible: Everything You Need to Know About Choosing, Using & Enjoying Your RV*, Fireside, 1997.

Banham, Reyner, *A Critic Writes: Selected Essays by Reyner Banham*, University of California Press, 1996.

Barker, Aldred F, *First Experiences with Motor Car and Camera*, Matthews and Brooke, 1911.

Barker, Aldred F, *Camping with Motor-Car & Camera*, J M Dent & Sons, 1913.

Beck, Roger D, *Some Turtles Have Nice Shells*, self-published, 2002.

Bedell, Mary Crehore, *Modern Gypsies. The story of a twelve thousand mile motor camping trip encircling the United States*, Williams & Wilkins Co, 1924.

Belasco, Warren James, *Americans on the Road: From autocamp to motel, 1910-1945*, MIT Press, 1979.

Bobbitt, Malcolm, *VW Bus Type 2*, Veloce Publishing, 2001.

Burkhart, Bryan and David Hunt, *Airstream: The History of the Land Yacht*, Chronicle Books, 2000.

Burkhart, Bryan, Noyes, Phil and Arieff, Alison, *Travel Trailer: A Visual History of Mobile America*, Gibbs Smith, 2002.

Burt, William M, *Volkswagen Bus*, Motor Books International, 2003.

Clarke, R M (compiled by), *Volkswagen Bus/Camper/Van Performance Portfolio 1954-1967*, Brooklands Books Ltd.

Clarke, R M, (compiled by), *Volkswagen Bus/Camper/Van Performance Portfolio 1968-1979*, Brooklands Books Ltd.

Clarke, R M, (compiled by), *Volkswagen Bus/Camper/Van Performance Portfolio 1979-1991*, Brooklands Books Ltd.

Cohan, Steven and Hark, Ina Rae, eds, *The Road Movie Book*, Routledge, 1997.

Cook, T, *Vans and the Truckin' Life*, Harry N Abrams Inc, 1977.

Cormack, Bill, *A History of Holidays 1812-1990*, Routledge, 1998.

Counts, Dorothy and David, *Over the Next Hill: An Ethnography of RVing Seniors in North America*, Broadview Press Ltd, 1996.

Darling, Jay N, *The Cruise of the Bouncing Betsy: a trailer travelogue*, Frederick A Stokes Company, 1937.

Drury, Margaret, *Mobile Homes: The Unrecognised Revolution in American Housing*, Praeger, 1972.

Dunlop, Richard, *On the Road in an RV*, American Association of Retired Persons, 1987.

Eccles, David, *VW Transporter & Microbus Specification Guide 1950-1967*, The Crowood Press, 2002.

Engel, Lyle Kenyon, *The Complete Book of Motor Camping*, Arco Publishers, 1979.

Estes, Bill, *The RV Handbook: Essential How-to Guide for the RV Owner*, Trailer Life Books, 2001.

Fagg, Christine, *All about Caravan Holidays: a guide to living on wheels*, Elek, 1975.

Fergus, Jim, *The Sporting Road: Travels Across America in an Airstream Trailer*, Griffin Trade, 2000.

Ferguson, Melville F, *Motor Camping on Western Trail*, Century Co, 1924.

Gellner, Arrol and Keister, Douglas, *Ready to Roll: A Celebration of the Classic American Travel Trailer*, Viking Press, 2003.

Groene, Janet, *RVs: The Drive for Independence*, Crescent Hill Books, 1997.

Groene, Janet, *Cooking Aboard your RV*, Ragged Mountain Press, 1993.

Hart, John Fraser, Morgan, John, Rhodes, Michelle J and Morgan, John T, *The Unknown World of the Mobile Home*, Johns Hopkins University Press, 2002.

Hibbs, John, *On the Move: A Market for Mobility on the Roads*, Institute of Economic Affairs, 1993.

Hollis, Tim, *Dixie Before Disney: 100 Years of Roadside Fun*, University Press of Mississippi, 1999.

Hulme, Kathryn, *How's the Road?*, self-published, 1928.

Hutchinson, Roger, *High Sixties: The Summer of Riot and Love*, Mainstream, 1992.

Jakle, John A, *The Tourist: Travel in 20th Century North America*, University of Nebraska Press, 1985.

Jenkinson, Andrew, *Caravans: The Illustrated History 1919-1959*, Veloce Publishing, 1998.

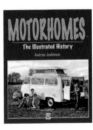

Jenkinson, Andrew. *Motorhomes: The Illustrated History*, Veloce Publishing, 2003.

Jessup, Elon, *The Motor Camping Book*, G P Putnam and Sons, 1921.

Keister, Doug, *Ready to Roll: A Celebration of the Classic American Travel Trailer*, Studio Books, 2003.

Keister, Doug, *Silver Palaces*, Gibbs Smith Publishers, 2004.

Kerouac, Jack, *On the Road*, Viking Press, 1957.

Kerr, Joe and Wollen, Peter, eds, *Autopia: Cars and Culture*, Reaktion, 2002.

Kronenburg, Robert, *Houses in Motion: The Genesis, History and Development of the Portable Building*, Academy Editions, 2002.

Kronenburg, Robert, *Portable Architecture*, Architectural Press, 2003.

Lackey, Kris, *RoadFrames: The American Highway Narrative*, University of Nebraska Press, 1997.

Lewis, Sinclair, *Free Air*, University of Nebraska Press, 1993 (reprint of 1919 edition).

Lidz, Jane, *Rolling Homes: Handmade Houses on Wheels*, A&W Publishers, 1979.

Long, J C, *Motor camping*, Dodd, Mead and Company, 1923.

McAdoo, Richard, B, *Eccentric Circles: Around America in a House on Wheels*, Houghton Mifflin Company, 1991.

McClure, Louis C, *How to Build Low Cost Motorhomes*, 1973.

McLynn, Frank, *Wagons West: The Epic Story of America's Overland Trails*, Jonathan Cape, 2002.

Meredith, Laurence, *Volkswagen-Transporter: The Complete Story*, The Crowood Press Ltd, 1998.

Meredith, Laurence, *VW Bus Custom Handbook*, Motorbooks International, 1994.

Meredith, Laurence, *VW Bus*, Sutton Publishing Ltd, 1999.

Miller, Alfred Dennis, *Motoring with a Trailer Caravan*, G T Foulis & Co, 1961.

Moeller, Bill and Jan, *Full Time RVing: A Complete Guide to Life on the Open Road*, Trailer Life Books, 1986.

Moeller, Bill, *RVing Basics*, Ragged Mountain Press, 1995.

Moon, William Least Heat, *Blue Highways: A Journey into America*, Atlantic Monthly Press, 1982.

Myhill, Henry, *Motor caravanning: a complete guide*, Ward Lock, 1976.

North, Arthur Edwin, *The Book of the Trailer Caravan*, Sir Isaac Pitman & Sons, 1952.

Noyes, Phil, *Trailer Travel: A Visual History of Mobile America*, Gibbs Smith Publishers, 2002.

Pallidini, Jodi and Dubin, Beverly, *Roll Your Own: The Complete Guide to Living in a Truck, Bus, Van or Camper*, Collier Books, 1974.

Pearson, David, *Freewheeling Homes (The House that Jack Built series)*, Gaia Books Ltd, 2002.

Perry, Paul, *On the Bus: The complete guide to the legendary trip of Ken Kesey and the Merry Pranksters and the birth of the counterculture*, Thunder's Mouth Press, 1990.

Peterson, Kay and Joe, *Encyclopaedia for RVers II*, 1999.

Pickett, Charles, ed, *Cars and Culture: Our Driving Passions*, Powerhouse Publishing and Harper Collins, 1998.

Porter, L, *How to Convert VW Bus or Van to Camper*, Veloce Publishing, 2004.

Primeau, Ronald, *Romance of the Road: The Literature of the American Highway*, Bowling Green State University Popular Press, 1996.

Rawlings, Irene and Abel, Mary, *Portable Houses*, Gibbs Smith, 2004.

Roggero, Alex, with Beadle, Tony, *Go Greyhound: A Pictorial Tribute to an American Icon*, Osprey, 1995.

Rosander, Ben, *Dreams on Wheels: Modern Do-it-yourself Gypsies*, self-published, 2002.

Rosander, Ben, *Select and Convert Your Bus into a Motorhome on a Shoestring*, self-published, 2002.

Schaecher, Steve, *Mobile Homes by Famous Architects*, Pomegranate, 2002.

Schaefer, Lola M, *Mobile Home*, Heinemann/Raintree, 2002.

Schwantes, Carlos Arnaldo, *Going Places: Transportation redefines the twentieth-century West*, Indiana University Press, 2003.

Sears, John F, *Sacred Places: American Tourist Attractions in the 19th Century*, Oxford University Press, 1989.

Siegal, Jenny, *Mobile: The Art of Portable Architecture*, Princeton Architectural Press, 2002.

Sims, Blackburn, *The Trailer Home, with practical advice on trailer life and travel*, Longmans & Co, 1937.

Slater, Shirley, *RV vacations for dummies*, Wiley, 2003.

Sparrow, Andrea, *Volkswagen Bus, Camper, Van & Pick-up: colour family album*, Veloce Publishing, 1997.

Spear, Diana and Hammond, George, *Square Pegs*, Hammond and Company, 1959.

Sweeney, M and Davidson, J, *On the Move: Transportation and the American Story*, National Geographic Society, 2003.

Theobald, William F, *Global Tourism*, Butterworth-Heinemann, 2005.

Thornburg, David, *Galloping Bungalows: The Rise and Demise of the American House Trailer*, Archon Books, 1991.

Topham, Sean, *Move House*, Prestel, 2004.

Townsend, Derek, *Continental Autocamping*, George Allen & Unwin Ltd, 1968.

Van de Water, Frederic, *The Family Flivvers to Frisco*, D Appleton, 1927.

Wallis, Alan, *Wheel Estate: The Rise and Decline of Mobile Homes*, Oxford University Press, 1991.

Walsh-Heron, John, *The British holiday caravan product: potential for overseas marketing*, British Travel Educational Trust, 1981.

White, Roger B, *Home on the Road: The Motor Home in America*, Smithsonian Books, 2000.

Wilkes, John, *How to Buy a Volkswagen in Europe, Keep it Alive, and Bring it Home*, Ten Speed Press, 1973.

Willemin, Véronique, *Maisons Mobiles*, Editions Alternatives, 2004.

Willmott, M and Nelson, W, *Complicated Lives*, John Wiley & Sons Ltd, 2003.

Wilson, Nerissa, *Gypsies and Gentlemen: The Life and Times of the Leisure Caravan*, Columbus Books, 1986.

Wolfe, Tom, *The Electric Kool-Aid Acid Test*, Farrar, Strauss and Giroux, 1968.

Wood, Donald F, *RVs & Campers 1900-2000: An Illustrated History*, Iconografix, 2002.

Woodall's Campground Directory, Woodall Publishing Ltd, 1985.

Wrobel, David M and Long, Patrick T, eds, *Seeing and Being Seen: Tourism in the American West*, University Press of Kansas, 2001.

Zeichner, Walter, *Volkswagen Transporter Bus 1949-67*, Schiffer Publishing Ltd, 1989.

Clubs

United Kingdom

The Abbey Caravan Owners Club
www.abbeycoc.co.uk

Astral Owners Club
www.icastralownersclub.co.uk

All Avondale Owners Caravan Club
www.aaocc.org.uk

All Year Round (A.Y.R.)
www.icayr.co.uk

Association of Caravan & Camping
Exempted Organisations
www.acceo.org.uk

The Auto Camping Club
www.theautocampingclub.fsnet.co.uk

Auto-Sleepers Owners Club
www.asoc.fsnet.co.uk

The Bambi Owners Club
www.bambiownersclub.com

The Barndoor Mafia
www.barndoormafia.com

Bedford CF Camper & Van Club
www.bedford-cf.co.uk

Bongo Fury
www.bongofury.co.uk

Buses with Attitude
www.buseswithattitude.co.uk

The Camping and Caravanning Club
www.campingandcaravanningclub.co.uk

The Caravan Club
www.caravanclub.co.uk

Caravanners and Campers
Christian Fellowship
www.cccf.org.uk

Classic Camper Club
www.brmmbrmm.com/classiccamper

Club 80-90
www.club80-90.co.uk

Compass Owners Club
www.compass-owners-club.co.uk

Conway Owners Club
www.conwayowners.org.uk

Cornwall Volkswagen Owners Club
www.cvwoc.co.uk

Dormobile Owners Club
www.dormobile.org.uk

Eccles Caravan Owners Club
www.ecclescoc.co.uk

Freedom RV Club
www.freedomrvclub.pwp.blueyonder.co.uk

Gay Caravan and Camping Club
www.gaycaravanclub.com

Geist Owners Club
www.geistowners.co.uk

Hymer-Club International
www.hymerclub-international.co.uk

International Caravanning Association
www.icaacaravanning.org

International Caravanning
Fellowship of Rotarians
www.rotarycaravanning.org.uk

KampWomen
www.kampwomen.com

Knaus Motorhome Owners Club
www.knausowners.co.uk

The Motor Caravanners' Club
www.motorcaravanners.org.uk

Period Classic Caravan Club
www.period-classic-caravan-club.co.uk

Rusty Bay Owners Club
www.rustybay.co.uk

Self-Build Motor Caravanners' Club
www.sbmcc.co.uk

Split Screen Van Club
www.ssvc.org.uk

Still Stoked
www.stillstoked.co.uk

Type 2 Ireland
www.type2ireland.org

The Type 2 Owners Club
www.vwt2oc.org

Volkswagen Owners Camping Club
www.vwoccgb.org.uk

Continental Europe

Autocaravanning France (France)
www.autocaravanning-france.com

Bullikartei (Germany)
www.bullikartei.de

Camping and Caravanning Club Austria
(Austria)
www.campsite.at/cca

Camping Croatia (Croatia)
www.camping-croatia.com

Caravan Club Finland (Finland)
www.karavaanarit.fi

Club Caravaning France (France)
www.clubcaravaning.com

Danish Caravan Club (Denmark)
www.dck.dk

Danish Camping Club (Denmark)
www.dkcampingclub.dk

Federation Internationale de Camping et de
Caravanning (Belgium)
www.ficc.be

French Camping and Caravanning
Federation (France)
www.ffcc.fr

German Camping Club (Germany)
www.camping-club.de

USA & Canada

Acadiana Ramblers
www.acadianaramblers.org

American Clipper Owners Club
www.americanclipper.com

American Coach Association
www.americancoachassoc.com

Beaver Ambassador Club
www.beaveramb.org

Bigfoot Owners Club International
www.bigfootowners.com

Boondockers
www.boondockingguide.com

Born Free Leap'n'Lions RV Club
www.bornfreervclub.com

Bounders of America
www.bounder.org

Bounders United
www.bounder.net

Buskatiers
www.buskatiers.org

Buses By the Beach
www.busesbythebeach.com

Camping Quebec
www.campingquebec.com

The Casita Club
www.casitaclub.com

Classic Winnebago Motorhomes
groups.msn.com/classicwinnebagomoto
rhomes/

Coachmen Caravan Camping Club
www.coachmenrv.com

Country Coach International
www.countrycoach.com/lifestyle/club

Colorado VW Bus Club
www.coloradovwbusclub.com

Discovery Owners Association
www.discoveryowners.com

Dolphin Club
www.dolphinclub.com

Escapees RV Club
www.esacpees.com

Explorer RV Club
www.explorer-rvclub.com

Families on the Road
www.familiesontheroad.com

Family Campers & RVers
www.fcrv.org

Family Motor Coach Association
www.fmca.com

Fleetwood Travelcade Club
Fleetwoddclub.org

Full Moon Bus Club
www.fullmoonbusclub.com

Georgie Boy Owners Club
www.georgieboyrvclub.com

GMC Motorhome Club Directory
www.gmcmotorhomes.com

GMC Western States Motorhome Club
www.gmcws.org

The Good Sam Club
www.goodsamclub.com

Go RVing
www.gorving.com

Gulfstreamers International RV Club
Streamers.gulfstreamcoach.com

Handicapped Travel Club
www.handicappedtravelclub.com

Hitchhikers of America International
www.hitchhikerrvclub.com

Holiday Rambler RV Club
www.hrrvc.org

Jayco Travel Club
www.jaycorvclub.com

Keystone RV Camping Group
www.keystone-camping.com

The Late Model Bus Organization
www.limbobus.org

Loners of America
www.lonersofamerica.net

Loners on Wheels
www.lonersonwheels.com

Mandalay Travel Club
www.mandalaycoach.com

Monaco Coach Owners Association
groups.yahoo.com/group/Monaco-Coach-Owners-Association

National African-American RV Association
www.naarva.com

The National RV Owners Club
www.nrvoc.com

NEATO Northeast Association of
Transporter Owners
www.neatoclub.org

Newell Owners Club
www.newellcoach.com

Newmar Kountry Klub
www.newmarkountryklub.com

Rainbow RV
www.rainbowrv.com

Recreation Vehicle Industry Association
www.rvia.com

Retired Singles
www.retiredsingles.com

Rexhall International RV Club
www.geocities.com/rexhallrvclub

Roadtrek Owners Club
www.roadtrek.com

The RV Club
www.rvclub.com

RV Consumers Group
www.rversonline.org

RVing Women
www.rvingwomen.org

RV Louisiana
www.rvlouisiana.com

Safari Motorcoach Clubs
www.safarimotorcoaches.com/owners

The Samba.com
www.thesamba.com

SMART
www.smartrving.net

Starcraft International Camper Club
www.starcraftrvclub.com

Streamline Royal Rovers
www.tompatterson.com/Streamline

Strictly Vintage 2s
www.sv2s.com

Sunny Travelers
www.sunnybrookrvclub.com

Teton Club International
www.tetoners.org

Tin Can Tourists
www.tincantourists.com

United RV Campers Club
www.unitedrvcampers.com

Vintage Airstream Club (WBCCI)
www.airstream.net

Vintage Birds
www.vintagebirds.com

Vintage Shasta Club
autos.groups.yahoo.com/group/vintageshastaclub

Vintage Transporter Owners
www.keepitstock.com
www.vtobusclub.com

Vintage Volkswagen Club of America
www.vvwca.com

Wally Byam Caravan Club
www.wbcci.org

Wandering Individuals Network
www.rvsingles.org

Westfalia Car Club International
www.westfalia.qc.ca

Wetwesties
wetwesties.type2.com

Winnebago-Itasca Travelers Club
www.winnebagoind.com/html/lifestyle/wit

Rest of the World

The Campervan and Motorhome Club of
Australia (Australia)
www.cmca.net.au

Camping Club Brazil (Brazil)
www.campingclube.com.br

International Register of Microcaravans
www.trikes.freeserve.co.uk/irom/list.htm

Motorhomes Worldwide
(Australia/worldwide)
www.motorhomesworldwide.com

VW Owners Club KdF of Japan
www.vwkdf.web.infoseek.co.jp

More

Bus Nut Online (USA)
www.busnut.com

The Caravan of the Future
www.tcc100.co.uk

EarthRoamer (USA)
www.earthroamer.com

Jenkinson's Caravan World (UK)
www.jenkinsons-caravan-world.com

Mr Sharkey (USA)
www.mrsharkey.com

Sleeping Spots (UK)
www.sleepingspots.co.uk

The World of Motorhomes (UK)
www.worldofmotorhomes.com

Acknowledgements

All the owners who appear in the book who were so willing to share their stories, opinions and experiences.

All the manufacturers past and present who have supplied imagery and information.

Paul Stafford at Draught Associates for his patience and dedication to the cause.

The Recreation Vehicle Industry Association (RVIA), particularly Jim Lubinskas.
The Family Motor Coach Association, particularly Robbin Gould.

Dorothy & David Counts
Rikki James
Martin Watts and the Classic Camper Club

Dormobile Owners Club
Escapees RV Club
The Good Sam Club
The Motor Caravanners Club
Wally Byam Caravan Club International (the Airstream RV Association)

Everett Barnes
Forrest Bone
Grant Dodd
Jane, Mark, Porsche and Morgan Edwards at Destination RV International
LeRoy Grannis
Kelli Harms at Winnebago, Inc.
Robin Hudson
Jini Keasling at Airstream, Inc.
Jenny Nordquist
Steve Pepper
Ben Spencer
Sam Worthington

All the owners whose stories it would have been so good to include but for which there was not space.

Tahani Nadim, Abby Dennis and Natalie A Bell at Black Dog Publishing Ltd.

The RVIA for allowing the use of the diagram on page 9.

And huge thanks go to Duncan McCorquodale for being both rock and publisher.

Black Dog Publishing

Architecture Art Design Fashion History
Photography Theory and Things

The authors have asserted their moral right to the work comprising Home away from Home The World of Campers and Motorhomes.

Written by Malcolm Bobbitt, Lars Eriksen and Kate Trant
Picture Research by Natalie A Bell and Abby Dennis
Designed by Paul Stafford at Draught Associates
Printed in the European Union

Black Dog Publishing Limited
Unit 4.04 Tea Building
56 Shoreditch High Street
London E1 6JJ

T +44 (0)207613 1922
F +44 (0)207613 1944
E info@bdp.demon.co.uk
www.bdpworld.com

British Library Cataloguing-in-Publication Date.
A catalogue record for this book is available from the British Library.

ISBN 1 904772 27 7

Overleaf: Dormobile marketing brochure, late 1960s.
Collection of Malcolm Bobbitt.